# FRAGMENTS FROM AN INNER LIFE

**Evelyn Underhill**

# FRAGMENTS FROM AN INNER LIFE

## The Notebooks of Evelyn Underhill

*Edited and with an introduction by*
*Dana Greene*

MOREHOUSE PUBLISHING
Harrisburg, PA

**Morehouse Publishing**

*Editorial Office:*
871 Ethan Allen Highway
Ridgefield, CT 06877

*Corporate Office:*
P.O. Box 1321
Harrisburg, PA 17105

**Library of Congress Cataloging-in-Publication Data**
Underhill, Evelyn, 1875-1941.
    Fragments from an inner life : notebooks of Evelyn Underhill / Evelyn
Underhill ; edited and with an introduction by Dana Greene.
       p.    cm.
    Includes bibliographical references.
    ISBN 0-8192-1600-3 (paper)
    1. Underhill, Evelyn, 1875-1941—Diaries.  2. Mystics—England—Diaries.
3. Anglicans—England—Diaries.  I. Greene, Dana.  II. Title.
BV5095.U5A3  1993                                  92-35312
248.2'2'092—dc20                                    CIP

*Printed in the United States of America*
by
BSC LITHO
Harrisburg, PA 17105

# CONTENTS

**For Lin Ludy**

*"In each generation Wisdom passes into holy souls,*

*she makes them friends of God and prophets."*

# ACKNOWLEDGEMENTS

My work on the life of Evelyn Underhill has spanned a decade, and the persons to whom I am grateful for support and encouragement are too numerous to list.

Those to whom I owe most for this edition of Underhill's notebooks include Sir William and Lady Katherine Wilkinson, who gave permission to publish them; St. Mary's College of Maryland for financial support; Gail McDiffett and Fay Campbell for help with manuscript preparation; and A. M. Allchin, Deane Barbour, Grace Brame, Fay Campbell, and Terry Courtret for insight into the meaning of these written fragments.

The encouragement of friends in the Evelyn Underhill Association, the Shalem Institute, Communitas, and Good Shepherd has been invaluable. My family—Richard Roesel, Kristin, Justin, Lauren and Ryan Greene-Roesel and Jacqueline Leclerc—has provided an environment of joy and affection which has made all the difference in my life. Finally, Lin Ludy, to whom this work is dedicated, has given me her wise love; my gratitude to her is without measure.

Dana Greene
St. Mary's City
March 1992

# FOREWORD

Those who pick up this book at random may ask themselves why we should concern ourselves with the inner struggles and despairs of a middle-aged Englishwoman living in Kensington in the 1920s and 30s. The answer is that when lived at a certain depth and with a certain intensity, the life of one can become the life of all; the life of all can be incorporated in the life of one. So what happens in one person can be fruitful and significant for others in many different times and places.

In the "Preface" to this book, Dana Greene makes a big claim for the significance of Evelyn Underhill's life and work. Its meaning was "to redefine religion and what it means to be a religious person." In the light of these pages, that claim does not seem to be altogether exaggerated, for they show us as nothing else does how what Evelyn Underhill wrote and said was rooted in what she was. They show the process by which one deeply interested in mysticism herself became a living witness to the reality of the mystic way.

As we read these fragments of personal notes and journals, we may at first be puzzled by their tone of passionate self-accusation. "I remain hateful . . . I am fundamentally a beast—but a beast that can't get over the ceaseless thirst for God." But then we begin to notice the contrasting passages where Evelyn speaks with equal vehemence of moments when her whole being is flooded with the sense of the nearness and reality of God. "Such joy that it sometimes almost hurts . . . a direct activity of the one Love, passing right through and vivifying one, like the sea waters supporting and passing right through a shellfish."

At times she is overwhelmingly aware of the reality and activity of God. Then suddenly she finds herself cast down into darkness, and into anxiety and fear that this may all be an illusion. "The universe seems cast-iron and the deterministic view the obvious one." She sums up her experience with the wonderful words "There has been some sort of mistake. My soul is too small for it; and *yet* it is the only thing at bottom that I really want." Perhaps the most moving of all the glimpses we get of her is that of her alone at night going out onto the roof at Pleshey, "just thinking Christ, too, prayed like that, high up alone, out of doors at night."

Like many in every age, she felt the total disproportion between the immensity of God and the littleness, the fragility, the weakness of all that is human. Her whole being, body, mind, spirit, shakes under the impact of the divine. Yet she learns to hold herself steady, and with the help of the whole Christian tradition, wonderfully embodied for her in the person of von Hügel, she learns how to find balance and calm.

Gradually she learns to reconcile the claims of eternity with the claims of time, to find the divine in the human and the human in the divine. The sacraments begin to make sense for her, linking the inner and the outer worlds. "Going to Communion this morning I saw so clearly all the suffering of the world and the self-giving of Christ to heal it—and that Communion and the life of union mean and involve taking one's share in that. . . ." And she is doing all this not in a convent or monastery, not in a rectory or a cathedral close, but sharing the daily life of a successful London lawyer with no particular religious interests, living in an elegant house in Campden Hill Square with the rush of westbound traffic streaming down the Uxbridge Road at the bottom of the hill.

When after Evelyn's death Lucy Menzies, perhaps her closest friend and collaborator, read these notes, she was astonished at the sense of conflict and turmoil they convey. All this had been hidden during her lifetime. On the surface Evelyn Underhill was the most delightful of friends, witty and vivacious, always accessible to others. T. S. Eliot, a frequent visitor at her home, describes her with marvelous precision and perception. "She gave (with frail health and constant illness) herself to many, in retreats which she conducted and in the intercourse of daily life—she was always at the disposal of all who called upon her, with a lively and humorous interest in human beings, especially the young. In her shrewdness and simplicity she helped to support the spiritual life of many more than she could in her humility have been aware of aiding." Now through her writings that support continues to be given. Her words become fruitful in the lives of others because they are the words of one who lives what she writes about.

This has happened above all in the United States where the Episcopal Church has wisely decided to place her name in the church's calendar, commemorating her life and work on June 15, the day of her death in 1941. These fragments from her inner story will continue to remind us of the price that was paid for the serenity and wisdom which shone out in her latter years.

To live a life in God has never been easy in any time or place. In the twentieth century, with its pain and darkness, its growing recognition of the manifest power of evil, it has been particularly difficult. But when life is lived at a certain depth, at a certain intensity, then the life of all becomes the life of one, and the life of one incorporates the life of all. Hence it is that Evelyn Underhill's inner world which was one of contrasts and conflicts, of darkness as well as light, can stand for the inner world of us all. She knew in herself the pain and travail of our time. Well might the words of Christ to one of her Russian contemporaries, also now numbered among the saints, St. Silouan of Athos, be applied to her in her shrewdness and simplicity: "Keep your mind in hell and despair not."

A. M. Allchin

# PREFACE

The life and work of Evelyn Underhill stand as testimony to the importance of the contemplative element in today's world. They witness not only to the need for self-reflection, but for transformation, for a life lived from a center from which meaning and purpose are derived. A prolific writer on mysticism and the spiritual life, Underhill redefined religion and what it means to be a religious person. Such a contribution is not easily made; in her case it was born in the crucible of her own inner life. It is the story of that inner life which is found in these notebooks from her crucial mid-life years.

Although she was lauded and acclaimed as a writer in her own time, remarkably little is known of Evelyn Underhill's private life. *Fragments from an Inner Life* fills that lacuna. These notebooks are the only sustained record of Underhill's doubts, failing, obstacles to growth, and gradual development of trust of her own experience. They have the immediacy and authenticity of spiritual autobiography and the detail that gives texture to her otherwise elusive life history.

These cryptic notes are important not only for the evidence they give of Evelyn Underhill's inner life, but also as an indication of her vocational shift from scholar of mysticism to exponent of the spiritual life for ordinary people, a shift that resulted in her pioneering work as a retreat conductor and spiritual guide for clergy and laity.

Evelyn Underhill kept these notebooks while she was a successful writer and a mature married woman in her late forties. On her journey to greater depth and self-understanding she sought the help of guides, the most important of whom was Baron Friedrich von Hügel, the Roman Catholic lay theologian. After his death she received the counsel of Walter Frere, Bede Frost, Edward Talbot, and Reginald Somerset Ward. The advice and inspiration of each of these men is attested to in these notes.

*Fragments from an Inner Life* is just that—unsystematic and private reflections carried out over a fifteen-year period. These notes must be understood within the context of Evelyn Underhill's life; used independently, they could distort and mislead. Taken together and in conjunction with her writings, they give depth and nuance to her life story.

These notebooks are important documents in the life of Evelyn Underhill, but they are also texts on the journey of the life of the spirit. In this regard these private documents assume a universal dimension.

What was the nature of Evelyn Underhill's life and contribution? And what do her notebooks reveal about her gradual growing into the Christian life?

Evelyn Underhill was a religious writer who was well received in her own time by Anglicans, other Christians, and those beyond institutional religion. Her friend T. S. Eliot said that her importance was that she understood the grievous need of her contemporaries for a contemplative element in their lives,[1] and at her death *The Times Literary Supplement* hailed her as "unmatched" by any professional teacher of her day in understanding the groping of the individual soul.[2] Underhill's corpus was a vast one, including thirty-nine books which she authored or edited and over three hundred fifty articles and reviews. After her death there was criticism both of her views on mysticism and of her writing on the spiritual life. But her work has stood the test of time. John Macquarrie, writing on twentieth-century religious thought, attests to her intellectual contribution. He argues that in the first part of this century there were only three women who made significant contributions to religious thought: Evelyn Underhill, the French Jewess Simone Weil, and the American Georgia Harkness.[3] The former Archbishop of Canterbury, Michael Ramsey, claimed that Underhill was important because she did more than anyone else to sustain the spiritual life in Anglicanism during the interwar period.[4] Fifty years after her death in 1941, there is ample evidence that she continues to be read. Her most famous book, *Mysticism*, has never been out of print since its publication in 1911, and today twenty of her books are still available. Whether examining the lives of the mystics, those she called "the great pioneers of humanity," or exploring ordinary life as lived by what she called "normal" people, she uncovers a movement of energy that is awakened and finally ends in giving birth to new life. In all of her work she reiterates in language that is immediate and accessible the central message of Christianity: that God loves each creature and that such love is transformative and life-giving. The way she came to that understanding and the development of her particular angle on that central message are the story of her life.

It is difficult to categorize Evelyn Underhill: she does not neatly conform to any one designation. The plaque affixed to her home on Campden Hill Square calls her a Christian philosopher. That designation is too narrow and imprecise. While clearly a Christian, Underhill was initially an agnostic and later a theist, and her sympathies went beyond Christianity. Her religious sense was of the broadest sort. Neither is the word philosopher correct; she is a philosopher only in the most ancient meaning of the word as a lover of wisdom. Philosophy connotes an occupation that is more abstract and more systematic than the one she undertook. Others have called her a mystic. She denies the designation and redefines the word so as to demythologize it. The mystic way is the spiritual way, open to all, participated in by the many, fully realized by the few. Neither does the definition of ecumenist capture her central contribution. Underhill always had a clear understanding of the unity shared by all religions, and although her last major work is a brilliant, intuitive defense of the validity and uniqueness of a variety of religious traditions, the word ecumenist allies her too closely with institutional religion. Underhill recognized the importance of institutional and corporate religious expression, but her principal contribution lies elsewhere.

From her early years she wanted to be a writer. One of the first glimpses we have of her comes from her seventeenth year, when she records her interest in literature. "When I grow up," she wrote, "I should like to be an author because you can influence people."[5] This early self-understanding is the truest one; above all Evelyn Underhill was a writer. At age seventeen she certainly did not know the direction of her influence, but the insight was there. In many ways the next forty years elaborated on that insight.

As a young woman Evelyn was an intelligent and lively person interested in the world. But she was relentless in her self-scrutiny. She accused herself of "selfishness, pride, conceit, disorder, moral cowardice, self-deceit, skepticism, thoughtlessness, revengefulness, exaggeration, want of truth, changeableness, double-dealing, teasing, unkindness, disobedience, dishonourableness, profanity and idleness."[6] This tendency toward self-scrutiny would plague her for the rest of her life.

Her interest in religion was minimal. At seventeen she said she believed in God but thought it better to love and help the poor than to love an abstract spirit she had never seen. Toward institutional religion she was, like her father, mildly hostile and suspicious. As she said, she was not brought up to religion. In politics she claimed she was a socialist, meaning that she supported a form of government that gives every class an equal status.

Of the Underhill family we know little. The barrister father, Arthur, and the philanthropist mother, Lucy, had only one child, born in 1875. Theirs seems not to have been a family of great warmth or affection. Evelyn was lonely both at home and at school. However, she did have a childhood friendship with the Stuart Moore boys, who lived one block away from her Kensington home. When the boys' mother died, Lucy Underhill and Evelyn took on a protective relationship toward them. At the age of thirty-two Evelyn would marry Hubert, the elder of the two. She seems not to have had other suitors.

As a young woman Evelyn engaged in bookbinding and writing. She had a number of unsigned essays published in women's magazines. In the early 1890s, soon after it was opened, Evelyn attended the Ladies Department of King's College in Kensington Square, a short walk from her home. There she studied languages, botany, drawing, and history, each of which was to have great importance in her life. Theology was offered at King's, but she was not interested, although she did read philosophy on her own from her father's ample library. Later she claimed that it was through this philosophical reading, especially Plotinus, that she came to God. While that is not untrue, it is only half the story. At least in part, Evelyn Underhill came to God, whom she called the Absolute or Reality, through her apprehension of beauty, particularly beauty expressed visually in art and architecture. Beginning in 1898 and continuing for more than a decade, Evelyn, oftentimes accompanying her mother, traveled regularly to Italy and France, visiting famous cities, shrines, and churches. On the surface, this activity was commonplace for women of her station. But it is no exaggeration to say that Italy changed her life. It introduced her to a reality she had not known in England. During those travels she kept notebooks in which she recorded her descriptions and sketched and painted what she saw. In Italy she discovered not only beauty, but herself.

"Italy," she wrote, "the holy land of Europe, the only place left, I suppose, that is really medicinal to the soul. . . . There is a type of mind which must go there to find itself."[7] "The place has taught me more than I can tell you: a sort of gradual unconscious growing into an understanding of things."[8] Underhill found beauty not only in the art and architecture of Italy, but in the great communal rituals of Roman Catholicism, which were so different from the religious world of England.

The theme of beauty was expressed in her first two novels, *The Grey World* (1904) and *The Lost Word* (1907). These are not good novels, but they illustrate the importance of beauty, explored first in nature and then in architecture, as the dominant preoccupation in her early writings. But the ardent and intense Underhill longed for beauty which transformed. It was this that led her to appreciate religious ritual. In Italy she always felt the outsider, closed out from the Roman Catholicism she loved. But in London she found, at least temporarily, a place where she belonged, the Hermetic Society of the Golden Dawn. She was a member for a little more than two years, probably leaving in 1905. It was within this community that she felt transformed and in touch with some greater reality. There is no evidence to explain why she left the Golden Dawn, but one can surmise from her subsequent writing that she began to see the dangers and limitations of magic. In "A Defence of Magic," published in *Fortnightly Review* in 1907, are found not only her concerns about contemporary magic but also the seminal insight for her first big book on mysticism. "It is the defect of all modern occultism," she wrote, "that it is tainted by a certain intellectual arrogance. A divorce has been effected between knowledge and love, between the religion and science of the Magi; and in the language of mysticism, until these be reunited the Divine Word cannot be born."[9]

While Underhill began collecting material on mysticism in 1904, she started to work on her book in earnest in 1907. It was a labor that would last for three years and would result in *Mysticism: A Study of the Nature and Development of Man's Spiritual Consciousness*, a book that established her as a preeminent authority on mysticism in the English-speaking world. The roots of this work were in her travels to Italy and in her experiences in the Golden Dawn. In pursuing mysticism as a topic, she took up a life's work. For fifteen years she would write biographical, historical, and analytical pieces on mysticism, as well as edit numerous mystical texts. Then for another decade and a half she would demonstrate to ordinary people how they too had access to the same reality as the mystics. Evelyn Underhill the scholar of mysticism became Evelyn Underhill the spiritual director, the teacher of prayer, the conductor of retreats. There are not two Evelyn Underhills but one; her life and work are of a piece, and they begin in earnest with the publication of her "big book." A project of this magnitude could not have been undertaken casually or without great emotional commitment; it was the events of 1907 that brought her to a decision to write it. *Mysticism* was born out of the very fabric of her life.

Evelyn was at a crossroad in 1907, a time of emotional and intellectual turmoil. She was a woman of great ardor, but she knew few who understood her religious intensity. Her parents were uncomprehending of their daughter's work and mildly irritated that it took her time, time better spent on them. Hubert loved, respected, and helped her, but he too was incapable of understanding her preoccupation with religious life. His work was marine law. He wrote some books on this subject and spent his time tinkering, fixing mechanical devices, and yachting.

In 1907 Evelyn decided to become a Roman Catholic, a move she had contemplated for some time. When she told Hubert, whom she was to marry in a few months, he was devastated. He protested that he could not have a Catholic wife. Evelyn agreed to postpone affiliating with the Roman church for six months, hoping to win Hubert over in the meantime. A few months after their marriage the Modernist controversy broke open. The Pope in a vitriolic encyclical condemned Modernism both in and outside the Roman church. In good conscience she decided she could not convert. She was forced to remain outside the church, without a religious home. For thirteen years she lived on what she called the "borderland." Ecclesiastically homeless, she committed herself to affirming the genius of the Christian mystics who, at least at this point, she believed lived independently of religious homes. Her need for intimacy and her sense of homelessness, both negatives, actually worked to propel her into creative activity. Turning inward, she claimed the thing she experienced as true: that the mystics, who lived most intimately with Reality, had something to teach everyone.

When Underhill's book *Mysticism* was published in 1911, there had been little written on this topic. William James had described mysticism in his Gifford lectures, later published as *The Varieties of Religious Experience*, and Dean Inge and Baron von Hügel had published on the topic, as had the American Quaker Rufus Jones. But Underhill's work was different from theirs. It was a five-hundred-page work of scholarship citing one thousand sources, but written with the intent not only to define and describe mysticism but also to convince the reader to take the mystics seriously. It was a work of scholarship and an apologetic. As such it was the foundation for all her subsequent writing.

The purpose of *Mysticism* is spelled out in its subtitle, "A Study of the Nature and Development of Man's Spiritual Consciousness." The mystics are examined as "the great pioneers of humanity" who, because they lived intensely with the Absolute, Reality, or God (she used these words interchangeably), were transformed. This transformed consciousness represented the highest expression of human achievement. Their lives also gave evidence of God's ongoing revelation in the world. That revelation did not happen once only in the person of Jesus, but was present in these "God-intoxicated souls." Their transformed human consciousness showed itself not principally in esoteric knowledge, nor in visions and voices, but in lives filled up with the object of that which they loved. Above all they were characterized by what she called "divine fecundity." They gave birth to new life in the world.

In an attempt to define mysticism she sets it off from magic, theology, and psychology and maps the mystic way through five stages of development: awakening, purification, illumination, dark night of the soul, and union. Underhill's schema has become the classic one for understanding the mystic way. Throughout she tries to show that mysticism is not something aberrant or abstract, nor an "opinion" or "philosophy" or "occult knowledge," but "that organic process which involves the perfect consummation of the Love of God."[10] It is "a movement of the heart, seeking to transcend the limitations of the individual standpoint and surrender itself to Ultimate Reality." In later work she writes that the mystics are those "who know for certain the love of God," and consequently they represent "the immortal heritage of man." They are not only "giants," "heroes of the race," but they are "kin" and "brethren." As the highest manifestation of human consciousness, they show the way for "normal" people who share with them a latent capacity for God. The mystics are different from other humans not in kind but only in degree.

In all of her work on mysticism Underhill's intent was to reclaim a part—she believed the richest part—of the Christian heritage and make it useful. The mystics, particularly the Flemish mystic, Jan van Ruysbroeck, and later St. Francis and the wild and eccentric Jacopone da Todi, provided the creative insight of her life; everything else followed from that. Her genius lies in the fact that she discovered this subject, recognized its power and influence, steeped herself in it, and wrote about it with elegance.

Underhill continued to write on mysticism after the publication of her book, even during the Great War. This was a difficult period

for her. Like so many others she strongly supported Britain's entry
into the conflict, but the protracted war, with all its carnage, forced
the question of suffering and evil to the forefront of her consciousness. What she found was that her disembodied and abstracted
sense of the mystic life was incapable of dealing with these harsh
realities. Later she wrote that during this time she "went to pieces."
She clearly knew that something was wrong and that she needed
help. She made two decisions: to enter again into the life of the
Church of England, and to seek the counsel of Friedrich von
Hügel.

It was these two decisions and the subsequent vocational implications which Evelyn Underhill would work through during the
1920s and 1930s, the period covered by her notebooks. Von Hügel
would be her spiritual guide from 1921 until his death in early
1925. After that she sought out first Walter Frere and then Reginald
Somerset Ward to fill the gap left by von Hügel's death. It is their
counsel with which she grappled during this time period.

The question of institutional religion was also paramount in her
concern, particularly during the late 1920s. Intellectually she had
come to realize that the institutional aspect of religion, one she
had deemphasized both in her work on the mystics and in her
personal life, was necessary to protect and preserve the central
mystical element of religion. She had given up hope of becoming
a Roman Catholic and only slowly came to feel that the Anglican
church could be home. Gradually she reached the point where she
believed that the Church of England was a part of the greater
church; she called it "a respectable suburb of the city of God." She
claimed that in Anglicanism there was "a great deal still to be done
and a great deal to put up with and the diet was often none too
good, but we are here to feed His sheep where we find them."[11]
She remained an Anglican because she claimed God kept on giving her more and more jobs to do there. In Anglicanism she found
the possibility of frequent Communion and a growing appreciation
of retreats, things which at that time she could have found
nowhere else outside the Roman Catholic church. Underhill came
to realize she needed institutional religion, but it was never her
consuming preoccupation—the experience of God was.

Her notebooks reveal that the question of institutional affiliation
is tied to the vocational question. Although initially uninviting, the
Anglican church proved to be a place in which she could serve as
a pioneer in the retreat movement in England and as a spiritual
guide to her generation.

The turning point in her vocation can be traced to her lectures at Manchester College, Oxford, in 1921. They not only gave her public visibility but also provided her with the opportunity to explore the spiritual or contemplative life as open to ordinary people. In these Upton Lectures, published subsequently as *The Life of the Spirit and the Life of Today*, Underhill examined the classical experiences of the spiritual life in the light of modern psychology. Although she continued to give lectures and radio broadcasts, the principal vehicle for dissemination of her ideas was the retreat. She made her own retreat in 1922 and by 1924 began conducting them herself. For more than a decade she gave as many as seven or eight retreats a year all over England. Almost all of these were subsequently published and constitute a significant part of her corpus. Conducting retreats and the "after-care of souls" became her principal vocation, one made extraordinary by the fact that she was a married woman who worked without the direct benediction of an ecclesiastical institution.

Her vocation, to speak to ordinary people of the spiritual life, the life of prayer and worship, became clearer as she pursued it. For her the spiritual life was "simply a life in which all that we do comes from the centre, where we are anchored in God."[12] It was not some discrete segment of life, but a consciousness derived from the experience of being rooted in God, a consciousness that came to infuse all aspects of life. This consciousness did not lead away from life and the world but to increasing engagement with it. The spiritual life grows out of the life process itself; it is organic. It expands to encompass all of life; it is inclusive. One knows it through participation; it is experiential. It makes one different in behavior and response; it is transformative. In writing of the spiritual life Underhill no longer used the concept of stages of development as she had in describing mysticism, but rather discussed it in terms of responsive actions that occur simultaneously: awe and adoration, adherence to and cooperation with God.

In her retreats and writing Underhill discussed the spiritual life as the life of prayer and worship. The purpose of prayer was to win one over to God and to help one see as God sees. Of prayer she wrote that its aim was to "stand alongside the generous Creative Love, maker of all things visible and invisible (including those we do not like), and see them with the eyes of the Artist-Lover."[13] Prayer ignites our latent capacity for God. Through prayer, one becomes what she called "a pure capacity for God." Although that capacity is fully realized only in the saint, it latently belongs to all humans. "The saint," she wrote, "is simply a human being whose soul has thus grown up to its full stature, by full and generous response to its environment, God."[14] The saints are on a continuum with all other humans. In many cases they are very ordinary "even unpromising" people when they begin. The saint is neither a "special creation" nor a "spiritual freak" but one who wants to be "filled up by God." "The saints do not stand aside wrapped in delightful prayers and feeling pure and agreeable to God. They go right down into the mess; and there right in the mess, they are able to radiate God, because they possess Him."[15]

The spiritual life has implications for everything one does. While Underhill herself took few public political stands, she understood that all of life, political and social, was influenced by this life anchored in God. "The spiritual life," she wrote,

> will decide the papers we read, the movements we support,
> the kind of administrators we vote for, our attitude to social
> and international justice. For though we may renounce the
> world for ourselves, refuse the attempts to get anything out of
> it, we have to accept it as the sphere in which we are to co-
> operate with the spirit. . . . Therefore the prevalent notion that
> spirituality and politics have nothing to do with one another is
> the exact opposite of the truth. Once it is accepted in a
> realistic sense, the spiritual life has everything to do with
> politics. It means that certain convictions about God and the
> world become the moral and spiritual imperatives of our life;
> and this must be decisive for the way we choose to behave
> about that bit of the world over which we have been given a
> limited control.[16]

Underhill's last major book, *Worship*, was published in 1936. This was a huge undertaking that demanded tremendous energy, something she increasingly did not have. Like her book *Mysticism*, *Worship* is an attempt to define what she called "the response of man to the Eternal." In addition to examining the elements of worship, she explores various of its expressions: Judaism, Roman Catholicism, Eastern Orthodoxy, the Reformed and Free Churches, and Anglicanism. In each she finds a particular genius, a particular ability to nurture a life of devotion and adoration. Each, she claims, is a "chapel" in "one cathedral of the Spirit." In this book she was an early ecumenist, expressing her ability to see with sympathy the uniqueness and value of these various historical responses to the Holy.

The activity of Evelyn Underhill's life abated in her last years as she was increasingly incapacitated by asthma. She took up another kind of work during this time, however, one that is little recognized and, for some, an embarrassment. In 1939, two years before her death, she became a pacifist. She joined the tiny Anglican Pacifist Fellowship and wrote for the Fellowship of Reconciliation. While she understood that many would view her position as simplistic and convict her of passivity, she remained steadfast. Her pacifism grew directly out of her Christian commitment. Although Hitler is a scourge, war is sinful and cannot be used as a weapon to combat his evil. "The real failure to respond creatively to the present mess is rooted in our impoverished and second-hand Christianity. We lack concrete, realistic faith and we fail to realize what unity really involves."[17] The sinfulness of war is the burden of everyone. All are accomplices. The only option was nonparticipation in the war and work to restore the world to the good.

Underhill claimed that pacifism was a gift, a vocation. The adherent was "a precursor of an age to come." Much like the mystic who dominated her early work, she saw the pacifist living out the full implications of the love of God and neighbor. That love was incompatible with war. As the air war rained bombs over Britain, Underhill continued to believe and trust. "In the dark hour of Armageddon," she wrote, "to adhere to the Eternal God and to help others steady their lives in the same way, must always be right."[18]

In June 1941, at age sixty-five, Evelyn Underhill died of a thrombosis. She was buried in the churchyard of St. John's parish in Hampstead. Her husband, who died ten years later, is buried with her. The nondescript marker reads: "H. Stuart Moore and his wife, Evelyn, daughter of Sir Arthur Underhill." It is a reminder of how women were defined in the early part of this century.

Fifty years after her death there are few things that recall her memory. There is the grave in Hampstead and her elegant house on Campden Hill Square. Her beloved retreat house in the village of Pleshey houses her Donatello frieze of Virgin and Child. Her crucifix graces the altar of the small All Saints' chapel in Canterbury Cathedral. It is her books, however, that speak most eloquently of her life. In them the desire for God that lured her on is most evident.

"In my beginning is my end," wrote Eliot in the *Four Quartets,* a seeming description of how the desire for God weaves throughout one's life. From Evelyn Underhill's beginning this desire is evident. It led her to architecture and painting in Italy, to nature and poetry, through the eddies of magic and the occult, to the allure of

Roman Catholicism. It burst forth in her exploration of mystic knowledge that revealed itself as born of love. It found expression in the editing of ancient texts, in biographies, and in the translation of religious experience into the language of ordinary life. It appeared quietly in the continuous "care of souls" and in their nurturing in retreats, and emerged again in her pursuit of worship, the most primitive response of awe and adoration. In the dark hour of war and death, God's meaning was hidden from her, yet she clung tenaciously to belief.

In the broadest sense the meaning of Evelyn Underhill's work was to redefine religion and what it means to be a religious person. Although religion may be connected to dogma, doctrine, institution, and moral code, Underhill believed its essential element to be the mystical, that is, the personal experience of the love of God that assures trust. To be a religious person was to be a holy person, one who lived out that personal experience of God, letting it move into every aspect of life. Hers was not a new understanding of the Christian message but rather its restatement in its most primary and clearest form. Her writing was the vehicle through which she expressed that understanding, but the understanding was born through conversion in her own life. It is here that her notebooks are important. In them is chronicled her gradual understanding of the meaning of the Christian life.

To read these notebooks is to encounter not a saint but a particular historical person with doubts and failings. They show her consciousness of her limitations, her deepening dedication to what she called "the vision splendid," and her growing commitment to vocation. *Fragments from an Inner Life* is the story of the love of God and the response of one woman to that love.

# 1

## INTRODUCTION TO THE GREEN NOTEBOOK
## 1923-24

*Fragments From an Inner Life* is a compilation of Evelyn Underhill's green and flowered notebooks, both of which are preserved in the archives of King's College, London. The green notebook is in Underhill's handwriting; the flowered notebook is in another, probably that of Marjorie Vernon with whom the Stuart Moores lived during the war. Evelyn died at Lawn House, Majorie Vernon's home in Hampstead, and it was Majorie who helped Hubert sort out Evelyn's belongings after her death.

The notes begin in January 1923, in the middle of the years of direction by von Hügel and several months after Underhill's visit to the retreat house in the village of Pleshey in Essex, where she had gone in 1922 at the invitation of her friend Annie Harvey who was Warden there. Von Hügel's direction and her experiences at Pleshey form the backdrop for the notes, which focus on her deepening commitment to Christian life, her decision to function within the Anglican communion, and her shift in vocation. In order to understand these notes, one must turn first to the circumstances that propelled her to seek the help of von Hügel.

Baron von Hügel was not Underhill's first spiritual director. In the period before her marriage she had appealed to Robert Hugh Benson, a convert to Roman Catholicism and a writer on mysticism, to help her decide whether to join the Roman Catholic Church. The fact that she delayed that decision because of her impending marriage to Hubert and because she never felt warmly toward Benson explains why his guidance ended in 1907.

For more than a decade Evelyn had no spiritual director. When she met von Hügel in 1911 she immediately liked him, claiming that he was the most wonderful personality she had ever known. Although they sometimes met at London Religious Society meetings, their contact was erratic. When *Mysticism* was first published von Hügel urged Underhill to make major revisions of her book.

She did not heed his suggestion. He continued nonetheless to re-spect her unique talents. "I have long felt," he wrote, "how many souls will be led right or wrong by yourself, with your rare charm of style, large knowledge of literature, and delicate interestingness of character. . . . You can and do reach more people than I can ever expect to reach myself."[1]

By 1920 Evelyn Underhill realized that she needed help. Beginning in 1921 she came under von Hügel's guidance (see Appendices I and II for her early reports to him). It is understand-able that she would choose him as a director. Although he was German by origin and twenty-three years her senior, they shared interests in mysticism, Roman Catholicism, and Modernism. He was a "scholar" and a "saint," she claimed. Aside from the mystics with whom she had lived intimately for almost two decades, von Hügel was the most formative influence in her life. Certainly she found him enormously helpful during this difficult midlife period.

Although Evelyn lived only a short walk from von Hügel's home in Kensington, much of their contact was through letters written between 1921 and 1924.[2] The fact that von Hügel was becoming in-creasingly deaf may have accounted in part for this correspondence.

Underhill came to von Hügel out of great personal need. The external circumstances of the war years had exacerbated her prob-lems. She wrote to von Hügel later on that during that time "I went to pieces." We know little of her inner life during that period. She was the preeminent English authority on the subject of mysticism and was giving spiritual direction to others. Yet this was a time of her "increasingly anti-institutional bias," when she drifted toward what she called an "inwardness." In short she had no religious in-stitutional expression, little sustained fellowship with other Christians, and no prayer life to speak of. She knew she was in trouble.

Underhill remained very productive during these years, except for 1917 when she produced only one book review. That year the Russian revolution occurred and the world war spread to include the United States. In the same year two of her cousins were killed in the war, and her dearest and most intimate friend, Ethel Ross Barker, became seriously ill with a terminal disease.

In 1918 Evelyn worked on a biography of the Franciscan Jacopone da Todi. Through researching his life she came to see the limitations of the neo-Platonic worldview she had embraced. In that same year she published an article on the future of mysti-cism in which she considered whether interest in that subject could be revived after the war. She concluded that it could, provided that it was connected to institutional religion so that it did not become "strange, vague and merely sentimental." These considerations of the limitations of neo-Platonism and the relationship between mysticism and institutional religion were the preparation for her decision both to reintegrate herself into institutional religion and to forsake her neo-Platonism for a more authentically Christian outlook.

Her decision to begin to function within Anglicanism was probably influenced by her discovery in 1920 of the Spiritual Entente, a secret fellowship founded by Sorella Maria, an Italian Franciscan nun. The purpose of the Entente was prayer among ecumenical members who attempted to live in such a way as to convince others that Christ was present within the various churches to which they had pledged themselves. Probably in 1920 Evelyn Underhill slipped back into Anglicanism; at this point it was an intellectual decision, one that she would gradually be able to accept emotionally. It was quite another matter to try to move away from the neo-Platonism that had dominated her thinking for decades. For this she went to von Hügel.

Certainly by 1920 she had come to see the limitations of neo-Platonism, this "excessive system of self-culture" which had as its final aim a "flight of the alone to the Alone." To her lights, neo-Platonism was incapable of dealing with the problem of evil. It offered no remedy for failure and grief and suggested only "lofty withdrawal" from conflict and violence. Although it could nurture adoration, it was not helpful over the long haul of life.

When Evelyn Underhill came to Baron von Hügel for direction, he saw someone who needed nurture, who had grown in inappropriate ways, and who needed to be directed toward new life. His diagnosis was that she was afflicted with "exclusive" or "pure" mysticism, that she misunderstood the spiritual life as some sort of self-development, and that she was emotionally starved. In fact these three maladies were interconnected, and their healing would come not through their direct purging but through a gentle turning toward God.

The relationship between von Hügel and Underhill was not one of equals. He admired her, but she adored him. Affectionate and caring toward her, he was nonetheless sometimes bracing and patriarchal. During their sessions she reported that he always made her sit on an uncomfortable chair facing the light. When someone complained about her severity in dealing with her own directees, she said: " You should see *my* old man dusting me down! You are all very lightly dealt with."[3]

Von Hügel had a profound appreciation for diversity among people, what he called one's *attrait*; yet his method of dealing with those who came to him for help was generally consistent. He was schooled in the writings of the seventeenth-century French spiritual directors, especially François Fenelon, and his own director had been Abbé Huvelin. Grounded in that tradition, he consistently argued for balance in the spiritual life and a curb on vehemence and excess of any kind. What he hoped for were "solid, simple, sober souls." His balanced spirituality was based on the simple discipline of a minimal devotional program which was always to be adhered to; a requirement to visit the poor; the reading of Fenelon; and the development of nonreligious interests. In Underhill's case she took up scriptwriting and gardening. Von Hügel's method was never didactic. His ideas were not so much "taught" as "caught." It was this method of "contagion," or teaching by example, which had great power to influence.

While teaching through his person, he also provided an intellectual framework, what he called "critical realism," a philosophy opposed to the subjective idealism he saw everywhere. At the heart of this philosophy was the notion that reality was twofold, temporal and eternal, a graded world of sense and spirit, nature and grace. In this reality, humans were "amphibious," conditioned by the sense world yet craving the supersensual or God. This latter tendency had atrophied but could be developed, not by denying the temporal but by immersing oneself in it. The finite was the sacramental, the way to the infinite and eternal. A philosophy that understood the interpenetration of the transcendent and the immanent was needed, and a religion which valued the mystical, the intellectual, and the institutional. While this "critical realism" was at the heart of von Hügel's contribution to modern religious thought, it was, Evelyn wrote, his "power of holding, and practicing together in all their fullness and variety, the pastoral and the philosophic sides of the spiritual life which made him, . . . without exception, the most influential religious personality of our own time."[4] Of von Hügel she said: "I owe him my whole spiritual life."[5]

Early in their relationship the Baron brought up the question of Underhill's ecclesiastical affiliation. Von Hügel hoped that if she could not be a Roman Catholic she could have a "Catholic" or "sacramental" understanding of reality, that is, a sense that the finite was the way to the infinite, that history and matter were in fact the way to God. This was a direct counter to her "exclusive" or "pure" mysticism. She needed, he maintained, "de-intellectualiz-ing," "or at least developing homely, human sense-and-spirit dis-positions and activities." For this he recommended work with the poor. This work, "if properly entered into, and persevered with," he wrote, will "discipline, mortify, soften, deepen, widen, quiet you; it will, as it were distribute your blood—some of your blood—away from the brain where too much of it is lodged at present."[6] These must have been painful and almost incomprehen-sible words for a woman who through dint of enormous effort had achieved remarkable intellectual success. To another directee von Hügel stated that an intellectual woman was "an abomination."[7] While he may have correctly sensed that Evelyn needed a broader and more varied emotional life and an appreciation of the histori-cal, material, sense-filled world, it is impossible to escape the fact that socially he was deeply conservative and reflected the nine-teenth century world that formed him.

In order to counter her "intellectualism," and ally her to the tem-poral and finite, he urged her to accept the historical nature of Christianity and to practice Christocentric devotion. Underhill con-sidered herself totally theocentric, but yet a Christian, at least in the Modernist rather than strictly orthodox sense. Von Hügel suggested that she try Christocentric devotion, to interwork gradually the theocentric and Christocentric, the mystical and philosophical, and the catholic and sacramental aspects of religion. While her prob-lem was intellectual, he believed its remedy was devotional and emotional.

Only gradually did Underhill come to appreciate this Christo-centric approach. Her indebtedness to von Hügel on this point is complete. "Somehow by his prayers," she wrote, "he compelled me to experience Christ. He never said anything more about it, but I know that humanly speaking he did it. It took about four months. It was like watching the sun rising very slowly. And then suddenly one knew what it was."[8]

While Underhill had gained a certain stability and balance on some issues by 1922, others were yet to be resolved. One of the first questions she brought to von Hügel was her inability to trust her experience: "Am I simply living on illusion?" She wanted certi-tude. Von Hügel rebuked her for this. "I don't like this craving for absolute certainty," he wrote. "God and Christ and our need for death to self are certain. At times you're tempted to scepticism (who is not?) so you want direct personal experience which is be-yond all reasonable doubt, but such an escape is not possible and

even if it were it would be dangerous for you. Don't build your
faith on these lights."[9]

Evelyn Underhill was an intellectual, and hence the desire for
certainty and fear of self-deception would remain with her. It was
her nagging sense of personal unworthiness, however, which
would be the dominant theme of the notebooks. Gradually she
came to see that her neo-Platonic view had no way to deal with
that question of human brokenness.

> ( I ) realize that only Christianity can meet the need
> of coming right down to one in the dust. . . . Plotinus
> can never have had to face his own beastliness. Neo-
> Platonism goes to bits when one gets really to the bottom
> and knows oneself unmendably displeasing to God.[10]

Underhill's letters to von Hügel and her notebooks are filled
with self-recriminations. She was particularly tortured by her
"claimfulness" in friendship. His diagnosis and proposed cure were
instructive. He suggested that her attachments resulted in part from
"the ardour of (your) natural temperament, but . . . largely from
the too intellectual character of your religion. . . . (I)f you get a
greater variety of homey emotions and activities into your religion, you very possibly will lose the hunger for *ardour* of human
affection."[11]

He urged her not to check her affections directly or be vehement in fighting them, but to turn gently to God. "In this way," he
wrote, "you will practice detachment with attachment."[12]

While preoccupation with her faults would never be entirely
eliminated, what emerged from this gradual focusing on God was
a new consideration of vocation. This deepening of the Christian
life and its vocational implications are two of the major themes of
her notebook for the years 1923 and 1924.

Like the relationship with von Hügel so too was her participation in the resurgent interest in retreats in the Anglican Church formative for her during this time. In 1924 Evelyn was asked by
Dorothy Swayne to conduct a retreat at Pleshey for members of
the interdenominational group, Time and Talents Settlement.
Underhill had attended her own first retreat at Pleshey in 1922 and
another in 1923, but conducting one was a different matter. She
worked diligently to prepare the addresses and enlisted her friends
to pray for her efforts. This retreat would prompt many more invi-
tations to give retreats in the coming years. Through this work she
became a pioneer in this new form of ministry in the Church of

England. It was this vocational commitment that helped her remain within Anglicanism. Although she continued to admire certain aspects of Roman Catholicism, she believed that the Church of England reflected the English mind and that it was her duty to make it Catholic. "I feel a great call to help on the renewal of sane Catholicism in England and am sure it is a work of God," she wrote.[13]

> It is obvious that people who can pray and help others too are desperately needed in the Church of England. And to leave that job because the devotional atmosphere of Rome is attractive, is simply to abandon the trenches to go back to Barracks. If all the Tractarians had imitated Newman's spiritual selfishness English religion to-day . . . would be as dead as mutton![14]

The vocational commitment had once and for all settled the denominational question. In 1925 Underhill would write: "Now the experience of God . . . is, I believe, in the long run always a vocational experience. It always impels to some sort of service: always awakens an energetic love. It never leaves the self where it found it."[15] Understanding of that statement was confirmed in this period. She experienced God in a new way, and a new service was awakened in her.

The years 1923 and 1924 were times of enormous activity for Evelyn Underhill. Her scholarly work and her public effort to speak on the spiritual life for ordinary people were now reaping a benefit: she was sought after as a lecturer. In 1924 she gave two lectures at St. Andrews University in Scotland and also lectured at York, Leeds, and Darlington. In the spring she was scheduled to deliver a lecture at the Conference on Politics, Economics and Christianity (COPEC) when her mother died and she was confronted with a myriad of family responsibilities. She published a few articles during this period, prepared an edition and introduction for Walter Hilton's *The Scale of Perfection*, and wrote her last book on mysticism, *The Mystics of the Church*, which was published in 1925. She continued to do spiritual guidance and began conducting retreats. She traveled to the continent with Hubert, yachted with him, and kept up a round of social activities that fell to her as the wife of a London barrister. She also became ill with bronchial asthma, a malady which would afflict her intermittently for the rest of her life.

It was within the context of this very full professional and social life that Underhill carried on the inner work described in the green notebook for the years 1923–24.

# 2

## THE GREEN NOTEBOOK, 1923–24

### Von Hügel in July *Hibbert:*
### *"Six Moral Marks of a Religious Man"*

1. Humility—our smallness in the universe is in God's hand.

2. Willingness to suffer—a genial heroism and impassivity in the ups and downs of daily life.

3. Sense of interdependence—charity to all in common—the duty and ability, not of loving the attractive but of *producing* it by "loving the unlovely into lovableness"—i.e., *creating love*—like that of God.

4. Truth—lovingness—a virtue very hard and on our level, apparently unrewarding, which is an earmark of our recognition of Ultimate Truth.

5. A richness and fullness in our sense of life and experience leading up to and only satisfied by the richness of God: changing the human thirst for full participation in mere Becoming to that for Being.

6. The poise which combines depth with happiness and issues in the paradox of Serene Suffering.

Underhill took these notes from von Hügel's "Morals and Religion," which was published in *The Hibbert Journal* in 1921. The article obviously made an impression on her. Since mid-October 1921 she had been under his direction. Although von Hügel always wanted Evelyn to be free to call on him, by 1922 he was quite ill. Reading what he wrote was one way she could absorb his influence. Her notes capture the essence of von Hügel's message in six abbreviated summary statements.

## January 1923

1. I feel I have considerably changed in this six months, and specially lately: but in rather subtle ways hard to describe. The main things are: a steady getting smaller and smaller, more and more completely *nothing* and dependent; yet more and more steadily at peace. I have almost ceased to depend on consolations or rush up and down the scale of feeling in the old way: but a steady line persists through fluctuations. Not $\mathcal{M}$ but $\wedge\!\sim$. More emphasis on will, less on feeling. None of the shattering sort of visitations for some time now; but a great sense of security, and on the whole, continuous inner happiness. Like Alice always nibbling one side of the mushroom—evidently the *right* side.

2. How to get purity of intention? Have I yet even seen the deepest roots of pride and self-love?

3. How to solve the psycho-physical tangles? The parallel between nervous states and religious sensitiveness? Best way to run one's devotional life when dim and exhausted?

4. What is the right line about mortification and sensual comfort or pleasure?

    a) Fr. W. Doyle's "look always for the most uncomfortable chair and then sit on it."

    b) "God made these things for you to enjoy, Dear Child!"—this might be stretched to condone adultery or anything and at least means sinking into the *most* comfortable chair and politely giving thanks for it.

    c) Just taking things as they come, with a bias towards simplicity. I have moments of violent impulsion to (a). (b) I think disgusting, though conscious that I sometimes yield to it. Is (c) good enough as an ideal if one really loves? I doubt this.

There *must* be something in the craving for pain; whether as an implicit sharing of the Cross, or as purifying and bracing up ready for what more may come?

The agreement between von Hügel and Underhill was that she was to prepare a six-monthly report of her progress and send it to him. These notes indicate that she did sense a change in her previous condition. Initially, she went to von Hügel because she felt unsteady and not at peace. She hoped for a more balanced attitude and one less dependent on feeling, something she was always suspicious of. Her increased steadiness was precisely the kind of result von Hügel had hoped for by his suggestion of a minimal devotional practice which could continuously be maintained. This practice included prayer, Eucharist, a yearly retreat, work with the poor, and the cultivation of nonreligious interests.

It was during this six-month period that Underhill had an experience after which she felt "called out and settled." She gives few details of the experience, except that she heard a voice, but insists that she is not hallucinating. She does not inform von Hügel of this experience until later in June.

Evelyn is preoccupied with her nervousness and how to discriminate between it and religious sensitivity. She is also concerned about the role of mortification. Father George Doyle, S. J., a contemporary devotional writer, urges an ascetical approach. While realizing that this might not be appropriate, she recoils from enjoying material things. While simplicity might be the answer, she is not sure that it is an adequate response of one in love. Evelyn is ardent, and her ardor can lead to imbalance. Von Hügel would remind her that mortification was not the central question—a steady focusing on God was.

## February 1923

Such lights as one gets are now different in type: less overwhelming in their emotional result: quite independent of "sensible devotion." More quiet, calm, expansive, like intellectual intuitions yet not quite that either. Thus yesterday I *saw* and felt *how* it actually is, that we are in Christ and He in us—the interpenetration of Spirit—and all of us merged together in Him actually, and so justly described as His body. The way to full intercessory power must, I think, be along this path. Quite half of what I saw slipped away from me, but the certitude remains: "the fragrance of those desirable meats," as St. Augustine says. Curious how keen all the Saints are about food.

Pascal's *abnegation totale det douce* seems to express the deepest craving—and that need have *nothing* to do with psycho-physical adventures. More and more I should like to get away from sensible consolations or at least their dominance. They are entrancing and overwhelming; but they don't really lead anywhere. It's the deep, quiet, mysterious love one wants to keep, and gradually transfer focus to the *will*. Sink down and down just grateful to be there—an almost invisible speck in the ocean, so the degree of blackness doesn't matter much. Vivid experiences are not over after all, as I fancied. But I don't really want them any more. Not perfectly sure they are pure and beyond suspicion. My own feeling state enters in too much: the other is not mine at all but an edgeless, penetrating love and joy—"the love wherewith the heart loves Thee."

In this entry, like the previous one, Evelyn finds that she is no longer dependent on her emotional response and is glad of it. She insists that her experience is more calm and expansive, both marks of authentic religious life for her. This experience was not merely intellectual. She *saw* and *felt* the relationship of Christ and the Spirit to the world. This brings a certitude that could not be affected by vivid experiences of either joy or sadness. The influence of von Hügel is evident in her desire to emphasize will, not feeling, and in her commitment to Christocentric devotion. These are months of real happiness, and for this she is enormously thankful to von Hügel.

**Lent.** I promise:

1. To try and accept and respond to all events without considering my own inclinations.

2. To try and avoid the spirit of criticism and especially uncharitable comments and thoughts. To watch this, and try to punish myself for all lapses: Speech to count double what thoughts do. *Never* let either pass.

3. To aim at calm and quiet both inward and outward.

4. Patience, sweetness, gentleness with *every one*, especially when rushed, hurried, tired.

5. Not let slip occasions for little acts of kindness, especially if uninteresting and unrepaying.

6. Total interior abjection and dependence on God.

*Note.* I broke *all* these—some many times.

My great, central need, more spiritual stamina. Am like a glaxo-baby—too long on these patent foods—may look plump, but deficient in bone. Want that bone hardness in my fibre, to stand firm on my feet when things get hard.

Evident here is Underhill's harshness toward herself. She feels that she is too pampered and petted, like a formula-fed baby, and that what she needs is real discipline. Only gradually will she come to see that in her own life discipline will follow from adoration of God. This subordination of discipline and mortification to adoration will become a hallmark of her spirituality. Unfortunately, it took her years to understand this for herself.

## February 13, 1923

For a moment, I saw the "Universe that thinks and knows." This solves all Christological problems in a flash. I suppose that *sort* of knowledge is what is meant by "spiritual truths spiritually discerned."

Underhill's Christocentric side had become stronger under von Hügel's influence. She will confirm this in her June report to him.

## February 18, 1923

This morning, not well enough to go to Communion. Stayed in bed: worried by feeling perhaps I was *really* well enough to risk it. Read Sunday prayers. Always fancied I couldn't *really* pray in bed—must kneel on a hard floor. When I'd finished, turned to God in prayer; and suddenly the Spirit of Christ came right into my soul—as it were, transfusing it in every part. How could I imagine this? I wasn't excited, but deeply happy and

awed. So intimate, all-penetrating, humbling. Lasted a
very little time. *Far* closer than even the best Communions. Yet the troubling part is, I remain hateful; only
with vivid efforts can I control impatience, even today,
after this, found people irritating and failed to be genial
and responsive. This would be the greatest argument
against genuineness; but on the other hand, it's nothing I
do—a pure grace—perhaps just because *I* do need it so.

Evelyn's illness was often the context for a powerful religious
experience. In this case she began to understand that the experience had nothing to do with her effort. It was unearned. Yet her
continuing "hatefulness" remains as the greatest challenge to its authenticity.

## March 16, 1923

Been through a black bit lately—over mastering
suggestion that after all, my whole invisible experience
*was* only subjective. There's *no* test—nothing to lay
hold of—I might right through have been deceived.
Once this lodges in one's mind it's absolutely paralyzing.
All the books say these things in unmortified beginners
are "very suspicious"—so, what *can* one think? So easy
to suggest to one's self—always reading these things—
and yet the reality doesn't match the books. One
*couldn't* deduce it from them—and it's on levels
infinitely beyond me. The only thing is to ask the Baron
and accept his judgement as *final.*

After it was over—but only set aside, not solved—
swing back to a divine inner peace, sometimes like a
continuous music but not distracting—just joy. Getting
easier now to make instantaneous refusals of pleasures,
etc., and dismiss them as soon as renounced—as if one
were being backed up, and *more* each time one makes
oneself do this. It's a more and *more* mysterious life. I'm
still far too critical, too dogmatic, fond of my own view,
not *nearly* gentle and humble enough in giving advice.

Went to see Eva Gore Booth. Found with joy and
amazement *she* had become vividly Christian. "What a
fairy tale of a life it is!" she said. Nothing *really* given in

any other way. Each new light she thinks must *at once* be handed on—that's the condition. *No* separateness. All vision of truth is in Him through love. Begin to get intercession right now—sometimes one can *feel* it act— Mrs. Rose and Miss Maud told me they *felt* it act. This is heavenly—gives one endless work to do within one's prayer and doesn't reduce the intercourse in the least— isn't mere petition at all.

Underhill was thrown back into depression by the suggestion that her experience was subjective and hence illusory. She brought this concern to von Hügel, who advised her to stopping thinking of certainty and to focus on God. For someone fully aware of the power of suggestion and psychic phenomena, this was easier said than done. She wrote to von Hügel later that there were times when she wished she had never heard of psychology. What was certain for her was her trust in his judgment.

She obviously experienced delight in finding the writer Eva Gore Booth a vivid Christian. Their friendship would result in Underhill writing an introduction to Booth's 1926 publication, *The House of Three Windows*.

Underhill thought extensively about the question of intercessory prayer. In a little book, *Degrees of Prayer*, published in 1922, she discusses intercession with great agility; it was problematic to her, however in the sense that it demanded complete love. She sees the great possibility for intercessory prayer, and has experienced its power, as have Mrs. Rose, one of the women she visits in the North Kensington slum, and Miss Maud Hance, her maid to whom she was very devoted.

**Passion Sunday:  March 18, 1923**

Today my God and Joy I felt and knew Thee, Eternal, Unchanging, transfusing all things, and most wholly and perfectly given to us in Christ—our in-dwelling with Him a Total Surrender to Thee—Thyself in all, the one medium of our union—at Communion to find and love Thee in each soul to which Thou hast given Thyself.

To know and find Thee, actually and substantially, in all nations and races and persons—*this* nourishes love and solves the intercession problem. "Not grace alone, nor us alone, but Thy Grace in us." To *use* and cultivate it. I think the parable of the talents meant this. How far beyond anything one conceived the mysteries seem to stretch now.

The more vivid the vision of Christ grows and the more insistent the demand for dedication, the more one can escape by this path from the maze of self-occupation. He draws, and we run after.

Her experience of God in Christ and Christ's dwelling in each person was made available in the Eucharist. This was of great consolation and would help her place her self-preoccupation within some larger framework. As she would say, it was because of the "vision splendid" and in spite of personal faults, that one was sent out.

### Retreat: May 4-8, 1923

*4th*. I've begun this retreat without much fervour— only just escaping another of those paralyzing fits of doubt. No clear sense of God's Presence—very tired— lately many obscurities and a sort of deadness. I feel less keen all round—not so ardently loving to the poor— sometimes quite an effort to be interested in them. But determined to slog on. Have got to start definitely learning God is in darkness for me as well as light. I've *nothing* at the present moment that the most ordinary small-beer piety couldn't contrive.

*Prayer.* The Good Shepherd leaning over to save the sheep, clings with *one* hand to the Rock, rescues with the other. So must we. Perhaps the secret of intercession is just this outstretching to others *while* we adhere to God?

Put my whole profession out of sight while here. This is my moment of Communion with God. I think He requires of me a willing entrance into the night of sense, detachment from consolations. Horribly difficult: still, my will is absolutely fixed.

*Short general examination.* Rows of sins, faults and
tendencies under Pride, Envy, and Anger—don't *see* any
yet under Lust, Gluttony, Sloth—probably because I'm
not yet *nearly* particular enough.

## May 6th, Sunday

The pain of obscurity went last night at Compline.
Afterwards I went alone on to the roof, in great peace
and acceptance though without vivid awareness—just
thinking Christ too prayed like that—high up alone, out
of doors at night—one comes closest . . . to His ideal
prayer. Gave a sense of complete smallness and peaceful
resignation: deep quiet and a kind of return to joy. Made
my Communion in great peace and surrender to
Christ—without strain—with great sense of the
completeness of God's coming down and into things to
us—all the Baron means by this came quite gently into
me as a solid truth—and after all *nothing* asked from
me, but love and a complete sense of my own lowliness.
The subtle realism of all the simplest things—if only one
could make people see that. Feel more and more the
best penitence for me is the general abjection and
dependence on Christ, not niggling about special faults,
but constant acknowledgement of falling short in love.

## May 7th, Monday

The silence ended this morning. Thou hast shown
thyself to me, O Christ, coming to me in the humblest
duties. Thou hast shown me Thy hidden life—Nazareth
and what this shall mean to me. This is the clear path
and right sphere of mortification for *me*. I shall reduce
even such apparent work for Thee as conflicts with this,
and try to fit myself for my service of humble acts of
kindness and love. This I have accepted and Thou hast
shone on that acceptance. I *know* it is right. Thy subtle
and mysterious presence is in this, and if I reject this, all
my work for Thee will be wrong. Keep this resolution
firm in me. This path, if I can keep on it, is full of Thy

light: it means love, repentance, satisfaction, self-denial,
faith—all graces in which I conspicuously fail. I promise
not to be deflected by people telling me I have a
"message," etc. I have nothing at all of value save what
Thou dost directly give and now Thou doest give this
priceless opportunity of real self-immolation. Since I saw
it, I am utterly and completely quiet and happy so I
know if I can do it, it is right.

*P. M.* I see clearly it's *total*, unconditional self-
annihilation which is asked of me and I know I shall
never do it—never, in this life.

It all goes back to the day I heard the Voice; all the
holy, deepened intimacy of this retreat is a following-out
of that really.

**May 8th, Tuesday.**  My last day.

*Fruits of this Retreat.* An enriched consciousness of
Our Lord. A little increase of light about intercession;
greater sense of interpenetration with other souls.
Renewal of joy, fervour, fixity of intention: fresh nerve
for difficult or dreary bits. Clear sense of mortifications
already here waiting for me, and resolution not to shirk
them and hunt about for others. Have been distinctly
shown my immediate duty—more home, kindness, love
and service whatever sacrifice of work or personal
preferences involved. The whole outlook, in the
moments of best vision, become wider, deeper, more
painful, more entrancing. Keep me, O Christ thus
centered on Thee.

This is the second of Underhill's retreats at Pleshey. Set in the
Essex countryside, the retreat house is at the edge of a small village with thatched cottages. Underhill loved the intimacy and
serenity of the place which freed her from concern with her professional life.

The euphoria of previous months has ebbed, but her resolve "to
slog on" is strong; she must adhere to God and help others simultaneously.  After a day at Pleshey she experienced a peace that she

sees as a direct extension of her experience in October 1922 when she heard the voice. She sees the need to ground all of her work in a dependence on God. The deepening of that love will cure her of her preoccupation with self. Her renewed sense of joy and clarity convince her that she need not seek further mortification, but must deal with all of life with greater love. After this retreat Underhill will ask von Hügel if she could make two retreats a year, rather than the one he advised.

## Points for Report

1. This strong feeling more time should be given to family claims—how far is this to go? I think it may have to go to real renunciations.

2. Obscurities—like a sort of stifling fog—far more painful than they used to be.

3. Consolations subtle and indeterminate. Many luminous, vague places in my theology. Experience of Christ still so subtle and intangible that I dare not risk damage by trying to draw a line round it.

4. Want of suppleness and of the spirit of acceptance. Still an egoist at bottom. Doubleness too.

5. Vocation—too many opportunities—can't take *all*—study and writing conflict with addresses, etc. Family duties. The poor. "Non-religious occupations." In *what* order shall I regard these?

6. Confess about automatisms.

7. Horrible renewal of temptations when nervous upset and desolation come together—morose, hostile to everyone, exasperated and generally vile.

These points and the self-examination that follows were probably made at the retreat and would serve as a basis for the report Underhill would make to von Hügel in the next month. In that June 1923 report she informs him of her experience of October 1922 when she heard a voice, first in Latin and then in English, which she says produced in her an experience of settledness. She understood "settled" in a general sense since many of her preoccupations remained.

Central here is her concern for vocation and her priorities, especially as regards her husband and her aging parents. These domestic concerns would increase in the following year. Although she
did not see theological matters clearly, she was more at peace as
regards them than previously. Her preoccupation with her own
faults remains. Since she believed that real Christians had a "gentle
suppleness and radiance" and that she did not, she again sus-
pected her own beliefs. Could a genuine Christian be an egoist as
she was? As to vocation, she was still confused and divided. Finally
when she was exhausted and tense, which was apparently a good
bit of the time, her old temptations to desolation emerged again.
All of these points were included in her June report to von Hügel.

## Self Examination

*Pride*
    I am critical—fastidious—rigid in my attitude to
uncongenial people—don't *try* to love—my hidden life
not *sufficiently* hidden—wanting terribly in abjection—
secretly think something of myself *for making* nothing
of myself—somehow allow people to think me
"spiritual"—an unbearable piece of "vileness when she
brings it into the presence of God." Lost in humility
lately, tended to harden-up, get spoilt again. Opinion-
ated. Not gentle and supple enough—risk of allowing
myself to feel I'm a teacher with a message, etc. Often
not grateful for opportunities of service, pick and
choose work and friends—don't take from God's hand—
resent circumstances that interrupt or displease me.
Notice neglect. Hate revealing my *real* faults. Like to be
thought well of. Allow Christians to think me a far better
and more established Christian than I am. They see I
care for Christ now, and I conceal what a disloyal cur I've
been. Am satirical, censorious. Enjoy derogatory tales of
others. This is a horrible vice in any servant of Jesus.

    Do things—e.g., service of poor—because it gives me
a nice feeling. Allow it to be known that I do these acts.
Talk too much about my slum people. Have generally
failed to cure ingrained ego-centricism. Don't put myself
out for people I don't care for. Condescending attitude
to family claims. Not sincere, to my own disadvantage.

### Covetousness

Coveted more spiritual consolations; hated having to descend to "ordinary piety." Wanted the graces I saw in others for myself. As to money, often give away less than I can *really* afford. Spend money on myself which would do more good in the slum. Buy things cheap without considering if this is justifiable.

### Envy

Envied L. M.'s spiritual exaltation. Was tempted to be jealous about Mr. R. These both disgustingly mean. Dislike the popular success of other people's "little books on mysticism." Discuss with enjoyment the faults and weaknesses of others. Often yield to the temptation to be amusing about them, repeat derogatory stories, etc., and don't seek for and show to others their good side, any how not steadily or consistently.

### Anger

Frequently impatient and exasperated—feel hostile to people without reason—reprove servants, etc., too coldly or severely—fail to make allowances or repress mere personal vexations—when nervous, irritable and unloving all round—intolerant—fretful, fussy, snappish even to those I love.

### Sloth

Get fed-up and don't strive to the uttermost in spiritual things. Slack in my watch on faults. Say the easy and showy instead of the quite true thing—don't exert myself to please people—don't *make* time for those who need and ask it of me, i.e., Jessie. Absurd to pray that Jessie may be comforted if I don't, at my own inconvenience, go and do the comforting.

It was precisely this sort of self-examination that would exhaust Underhill. Here she accuses herself of lacking humility and of being full of pride about her writing, lecturing, and work with the poor. She is covetous because she wants more consolations, and she lacks generosity toward others. This latter is particularly perplexing because her friends considered her enormously generous.

She envies the success of other devotional writers and the spiritual sense of well-being of her long-time friend and directee, Lucy Menzies. She sees herself as small-minded, quick to anger, and inconstant in her religious commitments.

Von Hügel immediately recognized that this type of long written examination was harmful to Evelyn, and in his response to her June report he urged her not to continue the process. Rather, she should gently turn to God. This would help her grow into a more general, though no less real, sense of her imperfections.

## May 12, 1923

The retreat had a wonderful tuning up effect; revived love all round somehow and deepened it on the religious side. Prayer gets more wonderful: a love, joy and peace to which there seems no possible end. Of course this heavenly consciousness will fade, but perhaps now I shall be able to feel it will come back. Even the most rotten little renunciations repaid a thousand-fold.

The result of this retreat was not merely that her former state of peace and happiness was returned, but that she learned that although her feeling of well-being might disappear, it would return. The need for consolation to give certitude was diminishing.

## Whitsuntide

More of these terrifying onsets of doubt when it all gets hazy and melts away and one feels, for a bit, it *can't* be real. The starving when away from home, *no* long recollections, no certainty of privacy so that one dare not lose oneself—all makes it worse. After a bit, one does get back through prayer to an atmosphere where it doesn't seem possible to doubt—and this seems more than ever heaven, after these tastes of hell—the enfolding, dim, penetrating love rushes in—but this doesn't *solve* the problem.

Evelyn's principal fear was that her experience was illusory. When she was under stress or unable to live her normal devotional routine when away from home, doubt reemerged. Even though she would regain her equilibrium, she would remain convinced that periods of doubt would recur. She reported this to von Hügel in her June report. His response to her was clear and unequivocal: you will never have an experience that will give you absolute certainty. He urges her to accept God and Christ as certain and work from that. While von Hügel proposes a way around her intellectual dilemma, he does not solve it. The question of intellectual certainty remains a problem for her.

## June 2, 1923

If I ask myself whether I am ready to face complete spiritual deprivation for the good of another—to lose all contact with Christ, all joy of prayer—give up my deepest life, e.g., that Hilda might find Thee—I can't do that yet. So I have not yet got *really* Christian love. And the question is, can one successfully intercede for the conversion of another, unless one is ready to pay, if asked, this price?

She inquires about intercessory prayer in her report to von Hügel as well. She believes that real Christian love demands intercession and that she is not yet ready to pay the price for it. One has to conclude that she considers herself a very poor Christian. It is clear that her emphasis is still on herself and her inability to live as she thinks she should.

## June 10, 1923

It came over me vividly at Communion today, that the whole of the life of Christ consists and always has in *nothing* at all but giving Himself—to every one who asks—pleasant or not—dingy beasts like me—*any*one— making no demands back, cultivating no heavenly joy for Himself—an eternal Risen Life of self-outpouring. It may sound obvious but when you see it, it's pretty overwhelming.

The importance of the Eucharist in deepening her understanding of the love of God is evident in this entry. In her last major book, *Worship,* she would explore this more fully.

## June 13, 1923

After a flat bit, mostly due to nerves and body, one rushes back to a strange indeterminate, almost *empty* blind joy, sometimes as if one's whole being poured out in a kind of wild craving towards God—quite in darkness but warm and inhabited—sometimes as if one stayed in a breathless little heap and was penetrated right through as if by a great wave pouring in. Joy, but with a queer anguish in it—but I don't utterly trust it or feel certain it's pure—there's something obliquely human; dreadful fear it has a "sensible" side. If one only knew how others felt, it would be better.

Here Evelyn shows both her strength and her weakness. She speaks of a craving for God, something she saw first in the mystics and then was able to acknowledge in herself. Nonetheless, she is sceptical of the experience, fearing that it is "sensible" and will not last. She remains isolated from others who might be able to help her evaluate this experience.

## June 20, 1923

Begin to realise now what the sacramental life is, and implies—that it just is, as St. Paul felt, "Christ in you"— His Spirit actually poured into one's soul, being in it, activating it, backing it up—always *there* to be appealed to. So, the strange intimate sense of union which comes now and again involves, really, a sinking down into one's own depths where He is. In loving Him, it *is* God one loves—more and more deeply I feel this.

It was precisely this sacramental side that von Hügel attempted to encourage in her. For one who was admittedly theocentric, this sacramental and Christocentric experience was new. This experience of apprehending God at the center and depth of one's own self would become central to her ability to speak of the spiritual life as "simply a life in which all that we do comes from the centre, where we are anchored in God."

In June 1923 Evelyn wrote a report to von Hügel.
(See Appendix III)

## July 3, 1923

O Christ, I *long* to serve you: and you won't accept
hard work and cleverness; you won't accept anything
but gentleness and love. And yesterday I was hard and
odious to poor Mrs. Lovell, and didn't try to console her
and wouldn't risk infection by stopping with her and her
baby and finding out if she was nursing it right. Just told
her *not* to come to work till she was out of quarantine.
Could anything be more vile? Right in the teeth of the
whole Gospel. I feel a cur, can't look at you, shut off and
bitterly humiliated.

In this prayer Evelyn juxtaposes her love of God and her unloving response to one of her household employees. Her position
was always that unloving action toward one's neighbor was an in-
dictment of one's so-called love of God. The result is a sense of
separation from God, whom she claims she loves.

On July 12, 1923 the Baron wrote a response to Evelyn's report.
What follows is her abstract from that report.

### Abstract

Account must be taken of: one's weakness, need of
precaution: inward *attrait:* outward duties: their
distracting quality: health. Begin by *needs* of soul and of
body, keep sufficient time for both, and for rest of time,
consider duties of one's position, and solid good one can
do, *without yielding to a blind zeal.* Do not cultivate
people to whom one can be no good, unless duty,
friendship, etc. oblige. Opportunity of mortification
doesn't enter in here—ample opening for mortification
is frequently against one's inclination; people one *must*
be with, and accepting one's *real* duties—never either
withdraw from or frequent people from motives of self-
love—do simply what seems best and agreeable to God
*even* if self-love be gratified; it will always slip in. Take

no notice of it, and go straight on. In a driven life, some periods of free and nourishing solitude *needed.* Suffer less and love more! Behave in church, etc. as best suits recollection but never be conspicuous; be free, don't worry, feed your soul so as to be more fit to suffer after.

In his report von Hügel urges no radical change in the program he has outlined. He believed that the gentle practice of habits he proposed would "simplify, expand, pacify, and feed" her soul. His concern throughout is for balance in her life to overcome ardency and zeal. She is to focus on what is before her, and to love more. The point is not suffering or mortification but love.

## July 18, 1923

*To be Followed (Friedrich von Hügel): Fenelon's Advice to Madame de Maintenon on Mortification*

Il ne faut point se faire une règle, ni de toujours suivre l'esprit de mortification et de receuillement qui èloigne du commerce, ni de suivre toujours le zèle qu'on a de porter les âmes à Dieu. Que faut-il donc faire? Se partager entre ces deux devoirs, pour n'abandonner pas ses propres besoins en s'appliquant à ceux d'autrui et pour ne négliger pas ceux d'autrui en se renfermant dans les siens. La règle pour trouver ce juste milieu dépend de l'état interieur et extérieur de chaque personne.

(One must not make a rule either always to obey the spirit of mortification and recollection, which draws one away from the world, or always to pursue one's zeal to bring the souls to God. What must one do then? Divide oneself between these two duties, so that one does not abandon one's own needs by attending to those of others or neglect the needs of others by withdrawing into one's own. The rule for finding this happy medium depends on the interior and exterior state of each person.)

Von Hügel frequently asked his directees to read Fenelon. In his response to Evelyn's report he asked her not to follow Father

Doyle's counsel but to read Fenelon's advice to Madame de
Maintenon on mortification. Generally speaking, Underhill did not
like the advice of Fenelon, but she obviously took this passage to
heart.

The following is her continued abstract from the Baron's report:

> Avoid everything bad for health—this will spare some
> suffering, but will only support and not flatter you. This
> is consistent with a way of life *sober, simple,* and
> therefore mortified in every detail *Nothing is more false
> and indiscreet than to try always to choose what
> mortifies us most*—this means ruin of health,
> friendship, work, all the talent God has given us! Zeal for
> mortification must never detach *either* from solitude *or*
> active life. These must be practised alternatively, not
> under a bushel! *even* though self-love may get some food
> from this. But hours of prayer and spiritual rest to be
> kept carefully. Never hunt for crosses—may choose
> those God doesn't mean for one. But accept promptly all
> those His Hand gives you. There is a providence in
> crosses as in the necessities of life. They are the soul's
> daily bread, and God never fails to give them. I entreat
> you to abide peacefully in this straight and simple
> course. In shedding this freedom, by an eagerness for
> sought-out mortification, you lose what God has
> prepared for you.

> *Be free, gay, simple, and childlike* but a plucky child,
> who fears nothing, says everything frankly, lets itself be
> led, can be carried about, knowing nothing, can do
> nothing, foresees and contrives nothing; but has a
> freedom and *hardiesse* unknown to adults. This
> childlikeness confounds the wise; and God Himself
> speaks by the mouths of such children.

Von Hügel's intent in all his direction is to develop solid, sober,
simple souls with staying power, at the same time characterized by
a freedom and childlikeness. In fact, many of his contemporaries
describe him in this same way.

## Special Directions for 1923–24:  Friedrich von Hügel

1. *Short* nightly examination—three minutes—no curry-
   combing or contrition for *possible* sins. General increasing
   habit of dropping *all* voluntary self-occupation during day
   and turning instead to God in Christ. This double practise
   is a substitute for drastic self-examination, and will
   gradually produce general but real self-contempt with off
   and on light as to particular faults, etc. These to be
   received gratefully: but not break-up recollections to
   brood on them.

2. *Purity of intention.* Be always ready to obey God but never
   anticipate His *possible* demands.

3. *Lights and experiences* may be humbly and gratefully
   received and used as *probably* of God, in so far as they
   brace and humble: but must always be regarded as means
   not ends, and even the most probably genuine treated only
   as helps to further flight from self and self-occupation.
   Even if all mistaken, God and Christ and need of constant
   death to self remain simply certain. Never build faith on
   them—this can only weaken, shrivel or puff one up.

4. *Mortification. Not* ceaseless deliberate *agere contra.* This
   intensity would feed my excessive vehemence and self-
   occupation. Object of right mortification to deepen peace,
   not shatter it. The Fenelon letter represents my correct
   ascetical type—supple, genial selflessness to be the aim,
   *not* fierce self chosen renunciations.

5. *Vocation.* General devotedness, not marked preponderance
   of *one* work or virtue, which would further feed
   vehemence. Help others reasonably but not to point of
   utter self-exhaustion. Try to improve *quality* of home
   duties. Real Christian greatness in being interested in *every*
   little nothing for love's sake.

6. *Rule.* Not to be fully kept in dryness or fatigue, etc.
   Minimum rule for these times: holidays, travelling, etc., i.e.,
   short morning and night prayers, examination, Holy
   Communion, and such bits of recollection as one can
   manage. *Full* rule for "fair  weather" only. When minimum

rule in force, some quiet manual occupation for my usual
time of long prayer. Fervour will then return more quickly.
Two short retreats a year; but without Confession or self-
probing. All advice and rule to be applied  generally and
with common sense. Extra Communions sometimes:
general practise, two weekly.

The sum of this advice is that she should have a balanced life—
in professional work, in domestic life, in devotions. She is to keep
a rule so as to focus more completely on God and others, but
everything is to be done with gentleness, especially toward herself.

On her specific queries regarding attention to her parents, he
urges her to improve the quality rather than quantity of interaction.
On her request for two rather than one retreat each year, he con-
cedes, but adds there should be no self-probing. He indicates that
she should send him a report in June 1924, if in fact he is still
alive.

### September 30, 1923

The appeal of weakness, need, sinfulness to Jesus was
and is immediate and complete: and so it must be to me,
if I would be Christian really. I cannot dare to go to Holy
Communion on any other basis but a general steady
aiming towards this completeness of compassion.

Although the person of Jesus is never a dominant theme in
Underhill's writing, his importance in her own devotional life has
increased tremendously since she came to von Hügel.

### October 14, 1923

There are certain advantages in being and feeling an
utter and complete beast—more than one meaning to
*O Felix Culpa.* At least one then avoids the *detestable*
temptations to self-satisfaction or spiritual pride, silly as
well as vile, when some trivial improvement is brought
to one's notice or worse when one observes short-
comings of others. Such thoughts, even though not
accepted, reveal a horrible, latent vileness. If only I

could be *quite* single-minded, and not observe with
interest my own state and actions.

Although Evelyn is still preoccupied with her own faults, this
entry shows a certain freedom about her own "vileness"; at least it
has some benefit.

## October 31, 1923

I begin to think that the most profound effects of the
Peace of God are manifested in the subconscious—it's
the quieting of this that delivers one from anxiety and
unrest. This accounts for the fact that though
consciousness of God is so often absent, the deep
hidden peace never seems really to fail, and wells up
gently when the mind is at rest. I wonder whether this,
which I have only just discovered by introspection, is
what the medievals meant by the "ground of the soul."

In this remarkable entry Underhill the psychologist meets
Underhill the scholar of mysticism. Underhill's ability to integrate
psychology and spirituality with her own experience is reflected in
what she wrote; this was one of her unique and appealing
achievements as an author.

## Advent 1923

This month of illness has been full of a sort of leisured
heavenliness—taught me a not intense and vivid, but
gentle, constant and peaceful dwelling in the Presence
of God. Quite easy to turn to external things without a
jolt and then back to Him again. Of course, not
contemplation or anything near it, but a very steadying
and enlarging sort of thing, and awfully sweet and dear!
What a span it is from the pure joy in God's utter
transcendence, to the intimacy of the presence of Jesus
in the soul—that coming right down to the bottom into
the dregs.

More and more I realize what the Baron means by
the "Otherness"—in this leisure one *can* get quiet and

recollected and make a little progress—my general life's too quick and packed with things—shall never seriously improve in prayer and vision unless I can get stretches of quietude.

Underhill's illnesses had for her their own positive effect; they gave her time for quiet, which she believed was necessary if her prayer was ever to deepen.

## December 4, 1923

Today, abruptly, in five minutes of prayer I *knew* the Ocean of Love—the "boundless living substance"— through me, and all of us, immersing us, one Love—it's true, "the plural is never found." Incredible joy—one feels in such a moment, one could never allow oneself an act or feeling below this—that anything but love is impossible—because it's *all* and all GOD—but I *shall* incessantly fall into separateness again. How wonderful that weak and rotten little creatures like me can see this even though one can't "sustain one's gaze."

Underhill seemed to use this notebook to record her experiences both of great joy and great "vileness." She describes the experience here as one of connectedness and belonging to the all which is. The nuanced difference is that she recognizes that this experience has been gratituously given and can be taken away. In fact it must pass away because one cannot bear it.

## December 26, 1923

Looking back on this autumn I feel I have chiefly learnt two things:

1. A deep and clear sense of the all-penetrating Presence of God and of Love as His deepest nature—or at least the nearest *we* can come to it: and so, of any decent thing we do as *not* ours, but a direct activity of the one Love, passing right through and vivifying one, like the sea waters supporting and passing right through a shell fish.

Yet, all the time, one remains one's own beastly self!
Great deepening and enrichment of one's sense of God
at times—but it slips away; I can't hold it.

2. More and more I realize, the union with Christ one
   craves for can and must be only through union with His
   redemptive work, always going on in the world. If I ever
   hesitate before this, the pain and stress it must mean for
   us wretched little creatures used as His instruments—
   then I draw back from Him and break the link. So the
   "life of supremely happy men" is *not* "alone with the
   alone"—it's the redeeming life, now and in Eternity, too,
   in ever greater and more entrancing union with the
   Spirit of Jesus ceaselessly at work in the world. Only one
   must have the quiet times, too, to consolidate that union
   and stretch-out the house of one's soul, and feed on Him.

In this beautiful summative entry Underhill describes both her
sense of God and the implications it has for life. God is Love and
as Love passes through one's flawed person; it does redemptive
work in the world.

The union Underhill seeks with God is no longer the neo-
Platonic one of "alone with the Alone." Rather it is a union
through love in and for the world. All love of God has vocational
implications that are redemptive.

## January 15, 1924

I don't think God will ever make me *good:* what He
wants is to use me as a tool, to reach others and do His
work in them. But in the end probably my sort is for the
dust heap. If His purposes are advanced and one does
what He calls for, one ought not really to mind this. I
doubt whether intellectual keenness and speculation are
ever fully compatible with sanctity. Meanwhile he is my
joy, and Eternal Life *is* a present fact and the sense of His
immense reality and penetrative presence keeps on
deepening; folds me up in prayer in a wonderful silvery
light and quietness and seems quite to extinguish the
desire and need for vivid consolations.

At last Underhill indicates some freedom from her preoccupation with her faults. The point is to be used by God as God wills; moral improvement will follow from that.

Although very fleeting, she indicates some doubt about how intellectual life and sanctity work together. This tension between the life of the mind and the spirit will remain with her. Yet the focus on sanctity is a new one. "Sanctity after all is the religious goal," she wrote. This theme will become dominant in the writing of the last years of her life.

## January 25, 1924

I don't improve *one bit* in charity. Today for a bit, suddenly and as it were forcing one into prayer, not a silvery light but a wonderful golden glow—and within this glow of God one sees Jesus. A sort of musical sense of adoration fills one then—nothing else at all but worship and delight. Had been to Communion feeling very dead and undevout two hours previously.

Underhill continues to swing between a sense of devotion and lack thereof. Her statement that she does not improve one bit in charity carries with it acknowledgement of her faults, but no preoccupation with them.

## February 8, 1924

Do feel lately a bit more as if I had got my feet on the ground. Recently that deeply quiet prayer, as if one just keeps still and the presence of God wraps one right up in a sort of velvety rest, comes of itself when one begins: though not of course always. When it does, there's no effort of over aim—it's all just as St. Teresa says. Complete, simple, and naturally-supernatural. I feel less and less distinction between times of prayer and times of activity within and for God: and this, though I remain very bad at aspirations, *horribly* blown about by temptations to exasperation, hardness and lack of charity, and generally not *one bit* better. But direction work is done now by something not me, which tells me exactly what to say.

In the middle of last night, when I was broad-awake,
something wonderful happened—a real disclosure—
convincing, complete. It's all completely gone but what
St. Augustine called "the fragrance"—but it showed in
the loveliest way the real relation between all our
symbols and images and the Reality, and that the
symbols and images *were* perfectly all right and truly in
it. A sort of infinite loveliness and colour and quiet joy.
One is *so* tiny and *so* much nothing—that the question
of one's own awful imperfectness doesn't come in.
There it is, in a sort of eternal regnant beneficence and
now and then one gets a glimpse.

As she becomes more steady, the old division between prayer
and action is now minimized. Although she finds no moral improvement in herself, she has a greater sureness of the loveliness
of God, and in the face of that her imperfections, while awful,
seem less significant.

## Ash Wednesday 1924

General intention for Lent—to try and learn to do hard
things for Christ. Remake last year's Lent resolutions.
Take particular care to consider the non-religious rights
and claims of others.

I think the chocolate-cream period is pretty well over
for me—seem being led away from emotional fervour to
a quiet but deepening adoration and self-abandonment.

Her Lenten resolutions for 1923 renewed here were meant to
give spiritual stamina and firmness to the "glaxo-baby" who had
fed too long on patent foods. Underhill was very busy during this
time; she needed such stamina. In addition to all of her lectures
and writing, she was occupied with preparing a retreat for the
Time and Talents Settlement to be given at Pleshey. For this occasion she prepared nine addresses, all related to the theme of sanctity as the perfection of love. In these she wove together prayers,
scripture, songs, and poetry. All this she recorded in a black notebook.[1] In addition to the addresses, she looked after every detail
for the retreat—music, altar preparation, Bible meditations. Her effort was immense.

## March 18, 1924

### <u>Conducting My First Retreat at Pleshey</u>

Had a tremendous circle praying for it. Maria, in Rome, prepared her soul with me. Baron told me to concentrate on knowing and entering into each individual soul and its needs, even while giving addresses—not just imparting information, but caring for and understanding each angle of approach. As soon as it began I lost my own prayer utterly—recollection or realization of *any* kind impossible. But was surrounded and supported by *something* which carried me steadily right through it without a quaver or anxiety—told me what to say in interviews—how to do the prayers with effect, even possessed me enough to put through the intercession services.

All in dry, thin, impersonal light but with self-giving to it. Ceased to count as an individual, felt completely a *tool* used by this strong unwavering power. Feel my whole horizon much enlarged and clarified by this experience.

*Object* of my life towards God is not, I'm now convinced, any personal achievement or ecstasy at all but just to make one able to do this kind of work. Self-dedication to His purposes for others—this is destructive of self-occupation and gives a most lovely free sense. Correctly, the retreat was finished by our prayer. Came back with immense peace and gladness in Christ.

The years of prayer and direction had changed Evelyn Underhill. She felt, she said, like a tool through which God worked. She had called on many, including von Hügel and Sorella Maria, the Italian Franciscan, to pray for the retreat. The result for her was clarity about vocation. The retreat was an important work. Certainly hers was a pioneering effort since retreats were a relatively new phenomenon in the Church of England, and she was the first woman to offer them. Her competence for this sort of ministry was recognized by an invitation in 1925 to address clergy and to give a retreat at Canterbury Cathedral in 1927.

## March 27, 1924

So wonderful tonight—as if one were plunged in that Ocean of Love—swallowed up—breathless with a sort of formless joy—all edges gone and yet it is distinct. So enraptured, it's hardly adoration, and in it, deep wordless communion with the Spirit of Jesus—the two sides together like that. Three-fourths of an hour. No words for it. Worried about mother, the Baron, everything: but it didn't matter—nothing *there* but deep inexplicable joy and peace. Almost intolerable in one way and yet so heavenly and so safe. Couldn't think or make acts or see anything clearly. It was like the Mirror (of Simple Souls) says, "She *feels* no joy, for she herself *is* joy"—all far too great and strong for one to grasp.

This entry is distinctive because it expresses not some surface change which is exhilarating and comforting, but, as she had written earlier, a quieting of the subconscious, "a deep hidden peace" that "delivers one from anxiety and unrest." Certainly she had reason for unrest: both her mother and von Hügel were gravely ill. The former had two months to live; the latter, seven. The loss of von Hügel would leave her without her most important human resource in the spiritual life. Athough she had never had a very intimate relationship with her mother, she must have grieved at the loss of her and what might have been between them. With her mother's impending death came concern about her father and who might care for him. It was a difficult time, yet on the deepest level she sensed an "inexplicable joy and peace."

## April 13, 1924

Tremendous ups and downs lately. All too dazed holding on light sensations during and after mother's death—inability to *feel* all the things people were attributing to me. Lost my prayer for a time, everything seeming to be resting on me. Went through all with a sort of iron steadiness. Necessary to make absolute acts of acceptance of all that may be in God's will—even giving our home up if it turns out needful—with determination to let *nothing* break my life of prayer. At first very distracted and on the rocks, but it has come

back now with several spells of quietude, just kneeling
at the feet of Christ quite close and in silence. Today,
such clear sense of being as it were a *cell* in a boundless
living web through which redeeming work can be done
and so closely linked with the others—Maria, Gwen, . . . ,
Anna, etc., sharing and exchanging strength and
prayer—being one's self but never alone now. I think
this is a bit of what St. Paul was feeling when he spoke
of the Mystical Body. These New Testament sayings so
much deeper and more realistic than clergymen think.
Somehow at the darkest moments, reading à Kempis,
saw entirely new meaning in the Cross and *how* little I
know of it really, and what mysterious deeps there are
waiting for me there.

Underhill was scheduled to give the COPEC Lectures when her
mother became ill and died. Her lecture, "The Will of the Voice"
was read in her absence. She says she just staggered through this
time, disconnected from others. After her mother's death she and
Hubert had to deal with the question of her father: should they
move in with him? Hubert was very opposed to this, and ulti-
mately her niece, Corisande Thorne, went to live with Sir Arthur.
The Stuart Moores remained at 5O Campden Hill Square.

She was determined through all of this to remain steady. What
gives her solace is her sense of connectedness to others, particularly those members of the Spiritual Entente who believed in intercessory or redemptive prayer. Her image, that she is a "cell in a
boundless living web," indicates her new sense of connectedness.
This metaphor, which she sees as like that of the Mystical Body,
has vocational implications. Both St. Paul and Thomas à Kempis'
*Imitation of Christ* help her to have some glimpse of what these
might be.

### Easter 1924

One comes to realize the institution of the Blessed
Sacrament as the first moment and sum of the whole
Passion—"He gave Himself in either kind." That is really
the whole story: and the same demand is more and more
completely made on us. As we receive, so we must give.
Only when we offer ourselves *whole*, taking all risks for

inner life as well as "body," for, to and in God, can we
even begin to understand the mystery of Christ. Only
then God begins to act in us and communicate Himself
to others through us.

Have such a distinct consciousness from time to time
of now being actually educated by God. And what I've
got, largely, to do is to let it happen. Makes the light and
dark fluctuations, etc. comparatively unimportant. When
hindered in prayer, etc., no need to fuss: but rather
accept this and all other difficulties gratefully as very
useful mortifications licking me into shape for His
purposes. I don't matter in the very *least*—this gets
more and more obvious if only one could remember it—
and the further this certitude goes the calmer and
happier I am.

Her sacramental and eucharistic participation has obviously
taught her something new. Absent here is a preoccupation with
her faults. Instead she comments on the fruits of her self-offering
to God: calm, certitude, and freedom. Once one offers oneself,
God can begin to use one as an instrument for work among others. But the emphasis here is not on offering her works and activity to God but offering herself. In a later piece on worship she
quotes à Kempis on what is wanted: "What ask I of thee more . . .
but that thou study to resign thyself to me entirely. What thing so-
ever thou givest me else I care not for. For I demand *not thy gifts
but only thyself.*"[2]

## Low Sunday

Humiliating discovery that I am not in the least *really*
surrendered and detached as I had hoped. Idea of having
to give up one's home and go to No. 3 with the various
contradictions of self-will and renunciations involved,
horribly hard to accept. Awful struggles and tension—no
light or distinct leading from God. No "holy indifference,"
just foolish dread of facing it!

Evelyn is referring here to the problem of her father and
whether or not she and Hubert should move into his home on

Campden Hill Place. Obviously she is very reluctant to do this for a variety of reasons, but she is concerned about her father's well-being. Evelyn always had an enormous sense of duty toward both her parents and tried particularly to please her father. If one judges by his autobiography, Sir Arthur's feeling toward his daughter was distant and cool.[3]

## May 10, 1924

Friday at Bermondsey after days of distraction, went into their tiny chapel with Dorothy Swayne and knelt down—and at once a sort of tide of adoration, not me at all, swept right through my soul and out the other side carrying all one's own worship with it in a rush of entrancing joy. These are the things so difficult to place or understand.

Going to Communion this morning I saw so clearly all the suffering of the world and the self-giving of Christ to heal it—and that Communion and the life of union mean and involve taking one's own share in that—not *being* rescued and consoled, but being made into part of His rescuing and ever-sacrificed body. And in the sacramental life one accepts that obligation—joins the redeeming spirit-element of the Universe.

Contemplations are the filling up of the reservoir for this—contemplative life *does* mean Gethsemane and Calvary. All the religious amorists hopelessly off the track. "Not as the world giveth, give I unto you!" How close we stand to the fringe of the supernatural and how its energy seems to penetrate every fibre sometimes.

Dorothy Swayne was Warden of The Time and Talents Settlement, a group that worked among the poor in Docklands, London, and for whom Evelyn had given the March retreat at Pleshey. Her meeting with Swayne must have brought to the fore again what she had said in the retreat and what she felt again that morning: that the life with God is not for one's consolation but to rescue others. The life of the spirit always ends in service to the world, service which meant death to self.

## May 21, 1924

Much, *much* more difficult than I thought. More tension, pain, weakness, liability to humiliating temptations, need of self-renouncement. Humbling discoverer of my own utterly unspiritual state. Can't distinguish between these fiery temptations which wouldn't *happen* if I wasn't fundamentally a beast—and sins. *Are* sins of thought as incitements to sins of deed?

But wonder and joy of Christ do flow over it somehow—one doesn't really matter—and however awful, somehow *is* redeemed by union in love with Him. How wonderful the willingness of Perfect Spirit to enter and unite with *things* like my soul. These truths seem emerging very faintly now.

In the same entry are two experiences that she finds belong together: the confrontation with her own sinful self and the indwelling of the Spirit in her. The "faintly" emerging truth is that she will always have faults and sins, but God enters nonetheless. The point is to accept this redemption and be filled with joy because of it.

## May 28, 1924

General tendency of this year—more and more work for God—less and less personal consolation. Much helpless craving for Him, more and more aware of my *hopeless* beastliness and inability really to love.

## June 20, 1924

I *am* fundamentally a beast—but a beast that can't get over the ceaseless thirst for God.

Again her two learnings are tied together. She is sinful; there is nothing she can do about that. *And* she has a "ceaseless thirst" or craving for God. This second realization, if developed, would diminish the significance of the first. Von Hügel had spoken of religion as a "metaphysical thirst" for God. He recognized this in Evelyn and tried to expand it in her.

## July 13, 1924

These besetting, even *nagging* temptations to all
kinds of unloving reactions, which I always hate yet
often can't resist—my whole impulsive nature in direct
conflict with all God wants of me—makes great interior
suffering. And then tonight such a deep, thrilling-
through, comprehensive sense of God—so fully
immanent and yet so distinct—as if one swings between
tensions and temptations and fresh light. I think the
weight of the Baron's prayers tends to press me more
and more into his sort of consciousness. Yet it all so slips
away when one tries to say it.

"Our vision of the Intercessor must be that of a giant
soul, striving with all the devotion of the mightiest love
conceivable to pass over to human need the Divine
resources."

Evelyn's swings between negativity and being filled up with
God are evident here. Von Hügel and his influence on her, as well
as his imminent death, are present to her. The quote sums up for
her the essence of intercession: it is the means by which Divine
Love passes over into the human.

## October 16, 1924

This morning in prayer suddenly I was compelled to
say: Take all my powers from me rather than ever let me
use them again for my own advantage. When I'd said it,
some strange and quite unseizable movement happened
in my soul—I knew I had made a real vow, a more
crucial act of dedication than ever before and shall be
taken at my word. There was a darkening, deepening,
and enlargement: a sort of "melting into the supreme."

This prayer of dedication is compelling in its authenticity, and
Underhill herself recognized it as such. It was, as she said, "a real
vow," in many ways a fulfillment of the premonition of which she
wrote von Hügel in 1921:

I see only too clearly that the only possible end of this
road is complete, unconditional self-consecration, and

for this I have not the nerve, the character or the depth.
There has been some sort of mistake. My soul is too
small for it and yet it is at bottom the only thing that I
really want. It feels sometimes as if, whilst still a jumble
of conflicting impulses and violent faults, I were being
pushed from behind towards an edge I *dare not* jump
over.[4]

## October 19, 1924

Again at Communion today that strong sense, that the
only complete life and real joy is in following Jesus
straight from the Eucharist to Gethsemane at least in full
intention and desire—unlimited and unselective self-
giving—redemptive surrender—*my* application perhaps
of Maria's *In tormento e travaglio per fratelli.* Those
and the Communion-dream must somehow go together.
Great peace—joy—certitude in this.

Sorella Maria, who had such a great influence on Evelyn,
claimed that in its essence the spiritual life involved "torment and
travail for the sake of the brethren." This was Underhill's experience too as recorded in her May 10th entry.

## Notes from Baron's Letters to Gwen

1. The helping of other souls means suffering and
   renunciation to the helper; a perpetual death to self. For
   the light-bringing soul brings his particular vision and
   conviction along with his own special outlook, tastes,
   determinations, insights. The soul helped can only take the
   light offered, as separate from such determinations, etc.—
   and will understand in quite different proportions and may
   even rightly reject what the light bringer holds most
   precious. This means much detachment, unselfishness,
   even humiliation. It means yielding up one's treasures and
   risking their being despised. It means forgetting one's self
   and fixing attention on the soul to be helped.

2. All souls are interconnected—hence we can penetrate,
   redeem, pray for, and suffer for one another in the most

literal sense; and can dedicate our physical suffering to the service of other souls.

3. It will deepen and strengthen the soul's life if we make it a practise to do a little *less* than our average rule when in consolation; and a little *more* than our average when dry. What matters and makes us pleasing to God is *sticking* to it, through all the changes of feeling, health, attitude, environment.

Another of von Hügel's directees was his niece, Gwendolyn Plunket Greene, to whom he offered his sane and gentle guidance. Gwen knew Evelyn and so it is appropriate that Gwen might share bits of his letters with Evelyn. Three years after von Hügel's death these letters were published. They remain the best example of von Hügel's spiritual advice.[5]

The thoughts noted here are not new to Evelyn, although her recording of them gives evidence of her desire to plant them more deeply in her psyche. What is necessary is that one have a rule that one sticks to so that one can take on the redemption of the world. This redemption is possible because all souls are interconnected.

Given these understandings, Underhill now had not only vocational direction and a powerful sense of belonging but also a freedom from the tyranny of self-absorption. In some sense a miracle had been achieved.

The green notebook contains no entries for 1925, a year that very much marks both an end and a beginning for Underhill. The year began with the death of her beloved Baron von Hügel. He was an icon who showed her God, a man who had "a massive passion for God." Now he was gone, and she felt bereft.

Evelyn Underhill the scholar of mysticism was to become Evelyn Underhill the spiritual guide. In 1925 *Mystics of the Church* appeared; it was the last book she would write on that topic. In the spring and fall of 1925 she was ill again, but she continued her work. She gave three retreats at Pleshey, a retreat for clergy at Liverpool, a lecture on the philosophy of religion at King's College, London, a lecture on prayer at High Leigh and at the Student Christian Movement Auxiliaries meeting, and one on social action at the Anglo-Catholic Summer School. One of her great joys in that year was meeting Sorella Maria in Italy. Her writing continued unabated. The following year she would begin to write reviews for *The Spectator* and become its religious book review editor, a position she filled for several years.

This transitional stage of Evelyn Underhill's life was over. She was fifty years old, a practicing Anglican, and a religious writer with a new vocation. She had gained through von Hügel a new strength and balance, and a whole new work lay ahead. She wrote to her friend Lucy Menzies: "(A) true contemplative vocation involves . . . the development of a spiritual force by which you exercise not only adoration, but mediatorship—a sort of redemptive and clarifying power working on other souls."[6] The events of her life prepared her now to work as a mediator, to bring others to a clearer vision of what the life of the spirit might involve.

# 3

## INTRODUCTION TO THE GREEN AND FLOWERED NOTEBOOKS, 1926–37

The period from 1926 to 1937 was one of enormous productivity for Evelyn Underhill. She wrote several books, including *Man and the Supernatural* (1927), *The Golden Sequence* (1932), and *Worship* (1936). Some of her essays and addresses were collected in *Mixed Pasture* (1933) and hundreds of her book reviews appeared in *The Spectator*. But her principal energies went into the retreats that she conducted on a year-round basis from 1925 through 1934. She continued to do spiritual direction and keep up a round of social activities and travel with Hubert during the summers. During this time she frequently had to deal with debilitating bouts of asthma.

The green and flowered notebooks chronicle her inner life after the death of von Hügel. For a year and a half she had no spiritual director. This hiatus is reflected in her notes, which break at the end of 1924 and do not resume again until 1926. During 1926 she began direction with Walter Howard Frere, Bishop of Truro. Although she was fond of Frere, she did not find his help totally satisfactory and at times sought the guidance of others, especially Dom John Chapman, the Benedictine abbot of Downside, Father Bede Frost, the spiritual writer, and Father Edward Talbot, a member of the Community of the Resurrection and one greatly influenced by von Hügel.

Evelyn met Chapman in 1929 and carried on a correspondence with him in 1931 and 1932.[1] She does not record his advice in the notebook, but brief entries are included on the advice of Frost and Talbot, probably from the period between 1929 and 1931 when she was most in need of guidance, something she did not think she was getting from Frere. Although Evelyn was frustrated with what she called "the thin gruel coming from Cornwall," she was attracted by Frere's simplicity and humility. She would be directly influenced by his interests both in the Russian Orthodox tradition and in worship. Although he was intellectual, learned, and devout, much like von Hügel, Frere was not von Hügel's equal. In spiritual direction he was much more tentative than von Hügel, much less forthcoming with his brief advice, and much slower in delivering it. Evelyn wanted strong direction, and Frere did not give it. It is unknown whether Chapman would have been her choice as a substitute. No choice was possible because Chapman died in 1933. In December 1932, however, Evelyn met Reginald Somerset Ward, through the good graces of her friend Margaret Cropper. He became her spiritual director in 1933.

Ward was an extraordinary man, a married Anglican priest with a family who gave up the security of a pastorate to become a full-time traveling spiritual director. His particular gift was his understanding of psychology and its application to the life of the spirit. Evelyn called him a "soul specialist." Although he was very different from von Hügel in his point of view and method of direction, she found them very much alike. Ward was a pacifist, and although there is no evidence to substantiate the claim, he probably influenced the development of her own pacifist position.

The issues that dominate this time of her life are different from her earlier concerns about self-deception and doubt. Reflected in the notes from this period are her "psychic storms." While she serenely conducted retreat after retreat and continued to give spiritual direction, she was herself afflicted by "incurable self-occupation" and a desire to "punish" herself, to "crush and mortify" her worst passions. What von Hügel had been able to help her hold in check was now unleashed in her psychic life. These notes chronicle her personal torment, her emotional starving, and her possessiveness, none of which she was able to deal with except through self-recrimination and punishment.

The period of the greatest "spiritual blackness" occurred in the summer of 1929 and seems to have focused on what she called her claimfulness and possessiveness of others. Although this was not a new problem, (von Hügel had attributed it to her emotional starving), it was exacerbated during this period. There was some problem with her relationship with Clara Smith, whom she had known probably from even before 1921.[2] Clara, who was not particularly outgoing, was for many years Evelyn's personal secretary. She was deeply religious and devoted to Evelyn and attended almost all of her retreats at Pleshey as her helper. Clara was probably one of Evelyn's directees as well.

It is difficult to know the exact nature of the problem between them, but there is an abrupt change in their relationship in about 1929. This was a great torment to Evelyn. Clara stopped attending retreats at Pleshey, and Evelyn records her fears of losing the affection of "C" (Clara) something she finds unbearable. This fear might well be connected to the fact that at some point, presumably at about this time, Clara became a Roman Catholic. As such she could no longer attend retreats or receive the spiritual direction of an Anglican. Evelyn notes that Clara was cool and indifferent, and others attest that they were less intimate.[3] Whatever the cause of the change in their relationship, they did remain friends. Clara worked to prepare one of Evelyn's last manuscripts for publication, and at Evelyn's death she wrote her obituary for *Time and Tide,* a journal with which both were associated. Evelyn's will contained a provision for a large sum of money to be awarded to Clara.

Frere was unable to help Evelyn with these problems, so she sought the assistance of others. The care of Ward was the most helpful. His diagnosis and cures for the maladies of the soul are laid out in his anonymous *Guide for Spiritual Directors.*[4] Ward diagnosed Evelyn as having a "delicately balanced psycho-physical nature" that needed moderation, variety, and the avoidance of self-preoccupation. This diagnosis and cure were very much in keeping with those proposed by von Hügel. Under Ward's regime of gentleness and balance the vehemence and harshness of the previous years began to abate.

During the period 1926 through 1934 Evelyn's inner turmoil was not directly evident in her work and writing. Although she berated herself for her faults, she somehow knew that her work was useful. In the summer of 1929, in the midst of what was the worst of her depression, she wrote: "And as to advising people, if it is put into one's hands, one just has to do it in simple trust that if one keeps as quiet as possible, God will do it through one and that one's own insufficiency does not matter much."[5] The same theme of trust in the midst of personal turmoil is taken up again a few years later.

> Yes! I think too it is possible to be used as a channel without feeling peace, indeed, while often feeling on the surface in a tornado! Nevertheless, the essential ground of the soul is held in tranquility, even through the uproar and every now and then the soul perceives this. The real equation is not Peace = satisfied feeling, but Peace = willed abandonment.[6]

An examination of Evelyn's retreats and writing of this period shows that she takes up some of the themes of her own psychic life. Her treatment of them is in fact very balanced, although she is incapable of applying that balance consistently to her own life. For example, "The Ascent of the Mountain from the Purgatorio," her retreat for 1931 published posthumously as *The Mount of Purification*, treats the theme of sin, which she sees as principally a negation. "What is called a sense of sin," she writes, "only has meaning because of the beauty and splendour and glory of Holiness."[7] Sin is a lack, an absence of what could be. It is "the self-regarding, irresponsible use of instinct which cripples the will, the real driving force of the soul, which is always, when pure, tending to move toward God—the supreme attraction, the supreme life."[8] Sin is a blockage against the action of God. Although various in its forms, it expresses itself in three ways: in energy set toward the self, for example in pride and avarice; in loving too much, as in lust and gluttony; and in loving too little, as in sloth and envy. As for treatment of these sins, Underhill argues that they can only be eliminated by developing an opposite quality. Humility drives out pride; tranquility eliminates anger; charity overcomes envy, and generosity defeats avarice. Her emphasis is not on "crushing" but on reorienting energy. "We are asked not to kill but to transform, reorder, discipline our ardour of life and love."[9] These words, written precisely at the time she was attempting to reorder her own love, carried this warning:

> But the passion of personal love and desire must not be killed or we cease to be human. It has got to be transmuted into its immanent energies, cleansed of the poison of claimfulness and taught the difficult paradox of detachment in attachment. The purity of heart which God asks is not the chilly safety of something that is killed in the refrigerator; but the serene and ardent love of Christ and His saints.[10]

Evelyn, who referred to herself earlier in life as a "white-hot Neo-Platonist," gradually became an incarnationalist. "It is not a harsh dualism," she wrote, "but a profound incarnationalism which requires us to set in order our physical and emotional life and subordinate all vagrant longings to the single passion of God."[11]

After years of activity and inner turmoil, in 1934 Evelyn decided to accept the invitation to write another major book. She consulted Ward and friends about the decision, since it would mean cutting back on retreats and other writing. During the late part of 1934 and all of 1935 she worked on *Worship*, which was published the following year. After the withdrawal from other acitivities of that year she scheduled six retreats for 1936, but attacks of asthma forced her to cancel half of them. Increasingly, as illness incapacitated her, Marjorie Vernon cared for Evelyn in her home in Hampstead. Evelyn did some lecturing that year and a series of radio broadcasts, which were published as *The Spiritual Life*.

The following year, 1937, was dominated by bad health. She had flu, asthma, and bronchitis, and Hubert's health was also precarious. She led no full retreats that year and canceled some of her lectures. In the fall she wrote that she was "having to leave off active work."[12] In 1938 she was awarded an honorary Doctor of Divinity degree by the University of Aberdeen but was too ill to go to accept it in person. Asthma forced her into the hospital and her physician ordered that her study, her workplace for more than thirty years, be stripped of everything that might gather dust. She finished a few writing projects and continued to write reviews for *Time and Tide*, but in many ways this was the end. There would be no more large writing projects, no more retreats and lectures, no more entertaining in her lovely Campden Hill Square home. She wrote to comfort her friend Lucy Menzies, who was also giving up her work. "You and I have both been allowed a good run of active work, but the real test is giving it up, and passively accepting God's action and work, and the suffering that usually goes with it."[13] Later she wrote: "These losses of liberty I think are among the hardest demands of the Lord. At least I feel them so, but perhaps they are meant to drive us bit by bit into the solitude with Him, which He requires of us."[14]

The year 1939 brought more illness to both Evelyn and Hubert as well as the death of her father at age eighty-eight. At this point she was an avowed pacifist and wrote in support of that position. A small prayer group was formed under her guidance, and she continued to write letters of direction to its members for a year or so. But the end was near.

Little is known of her inner life after 1937, when these fragments end. In that year she began a correspondence with the prioress of the Carmelite convent in Exmouth, a Sister Mary of St. John. In some ways the prioress filled the role of confidant and supporter, much as Ethel Barker, Sorella Maria, and Laura Rose had. Although only the nun's side of the correspondence is extant, the reader can gather that Evelyn's vehemence and self-exacting attitude is in abatement, but has not disappeared. Much as von Hügel and Ward, the prioress urged Evelyn to stop dwelling on her defects and trust in God. Apparently the nun found the same preoccupation with personal faults in Marjorie Vernon, who also corresponded with her. "I think," the nun wrote to Evelyn, her "step-daughter," "both you and Mrs. Vernon are far too occupied in making 'self' such a presentable person."[15]

On June 15, 1941, Evelyn Underhill died. The turmoil of her inner life was over. What remained was the evidence of her sustained and lifelong effort to focus on God. Her life and her work stand as testimony to what Blake's lines proclaim:

> *We are put on earth*
> *for a little space*
> *To learn to endure*
> *The beams of Love.*

She tried to endure the beams of God's love, witnessing to them as she could.

# 4

## THE GREEN AND
## FLOWERED NOTEBOOKS, 1926-37

### Holy Week 1926

Fifteen months without direction and with a good deal
of ill health and spiritual flatness. General overhaul to be
attempted now, completed at next retreat and condensed
results sent if necessary to Bishop of Truro.

Released to some extent from furious temptations to
jealousy and claimfulness. These may press more in the
future, must be prepared for severe-ish testing in these
directions.

Feel definitely now called to more sacrificial life—
union *can* only be in the Cross. Very difficult to actualize
in practise. Too soft about my health. Incurably self-
occupied. Restless in mind—seldom truly recollected.
Feel more and more one knows *nothing*.

Evelyn continued to write, lead retreats, and give spiritual direction, even without guidance for herself. She suspects that she is
too easy on herself regarding her health, and is frustrated about
her ongoing self-occupation. She notes a spiritual flatness and has
a premonition that her possessiveness, which at the moment
seems under control, will, in fact, become more dominant. She will
turn to the esteemed and kindly Bishop Frere for help.

### Notes Made in Retreat, May 1926

1. In all things where free choice is offered me, my use
   or renunciation of things and conditions must be
   governed by the question whether they are favourable
   or inimical to my service of God. This will *include*
   their direct effect on my soul's life; and more besides.

2. I must desire and elect only such things as best contribute to this final end of a life of adoration and service. Of each choice offered me, I must ask: how does this help, how does this hinder, the one aim? Apart from this consideration I must be indifferent to pain/pleasure, success/failure, and so forth. First quality required: absolute and equable Patience.

3. My own improvement and my ultimate state, my work in other souls, and which souls I shall help; all this shall never be self-chosen, but entirely determined by God. "Our activity spoils all, when it precedes the divine action instead of following it."

4. My own place in the spiritual universe, though minute, is yet unique. The work that I have to do and can do is my own, and no one else's. *This* work, in *this* place, can satisfy God and procure my sanctification, if done with purity and generosity and without self-love. If it fails to effect this, the fault is *mine*.

5. It is *essential* that I do full justice to the ordinary domestic bits of my life, as equally given me by God with the rest. These are direct instruments of mortification to all my worst passions: impatience, pride, self-will, uncharitableness, egotism, claimfulness. Must respond to *all* the people He puts in my life, so far as I can—not limit sympathy to the ones I like. Work out on the material He provides— the central principles of love, sympathy, abnegation and forgiveness.

6. Since my faults, and the difficulties which keep me back most, are those connected with social and domestic contacts, the humble fulfillment of all duties on this side of life, steady effort at gentleness, pliability, and self-forgetfulness, uncritical affection and sympathy, *immediate* ascetic aim.

7. I am as much required to be a Christian wife-daughter- mistress-friend, as to be a writer on religion and director of souls. Must combat persistent self-

occupation by forcing myself to enter into interests of others, however alien from my own.

8. All distinct failures in love: harshness, moroseness, intolerance, resentfulness, uncharitableness; to be punished by first available humiliating or distasteful act; remember I have *no* rights, status, or claim on consideration.

9. God in this Retreat has given me a clear view of my faults, and also of my call to His absolute service. It is *imperative* that I undertake the serious and painful purification of my unmortified nature hour by hour and day by day, and allow myself *no* quarter, *no* excuses under the needs of health, nerves, and temperament.

10. I see that it *is* possible to become such that Christ can act in and through one in utter peace and steadiness: O that this should be the final aim set before my soul, the raison d'être of all practices and mortifications, and the object of the sacramental life.

## Practical Measures

More patient, equable, sympathetic interest in my poor people; especially unrewarding ones. *Not* forget sweets for the children. Get more families if possible. More gentle and patient with the servants. Show approval when they do well: not give sharp orders.

Consider looking after Aunt E. a privilege for Christ; not a bore to be groused about. Constantly remember obligation of love and sympathy to *all*, as a transmitting instrument of the Love of God.

More frequent use of aspirations; especially the Holy Name. More careful observance of Rule.

Evelyn is clear that what she desires is a singleminded focus for her life—one aim that catches up all of her activity, uniting it and making it dedicated and holy. She sees her most difficult problem to be associated with the emotional demands of her domestic life, that is those made by Hubert, her parents, and Aunt Elizabeth, Arthur Underhill's sister. She berates herself that she is not interested in their concerns and admonishes herself to get interested. It should be noted that they are not particularly interested in her concerns either.

Whatever her growth in self-understanding, she remains harsh toward herself. She speaks of desiring humiliation for her faults. She wants no excuses, no pardon, no mercy.

## Letter to Bishop Frere Late 1926

My dear Director,

You were kind enough to say that I might write when I wanted to, and the result of the leisure of the holidays is that there are one or two points I would very much like to put before you. Very likely they are not worth your attention. In that case of course I shan't expect any answer and anyhow it is only a case of feeling easier if I have your authority just to go on or make a change.

1. This is in the nature of a confession. Since your last letter I really have tried to avoid hovering over faults etc. But sometimes things jump out at one. And I've been horrified lately to find I've slipped into a wickedness against which I really *did* think I was on my guard—self-will and love of power in direction work. In the queer way things happen, within two days four of my usually docile children resisted or acted against my advice in various ways, or preferred the guidance of others—and this, when on my own firmly held principles I *ought* to have accepted quite calmly, as a matter of fact I minded very much indeed. I really am ashamed to tell you this but must— because if self-will and self-love have got in *here*, it's fatal, isn't it? Nothing could be worse and some really severe measures must be taken.

2. The other point is a good deal more intimate and if I hadn't been to _____ I don't think I should have ventured to speak about it. But after that I knew you would understand and not think it awful. Until about

five years ago I had never had any personal experience of our Lord: I didn't know what it meant. I was a convinced theocentric, thought most Christocentric language and practice sentimental and superstitious and was very handy with shallow psychological explanations of it. I had from time to time what seemed to be vivid experiences of God, from the time of my conversion from agnosticism ( about twenty years ago now). This position I thought to be that of a broad-minded and intelligent Christian, but when, after a severe spiritual smash and partial recovery, I went to the Baron, he said I wasn't much better than a Unitarian! Somehow by his prayers or something he *compelled* me to experience Christ. He never said anything more about it—but I know humanly speaking he did it. It took about four months—it was like watching the sun rise very slowly—and then suddenly one knew what it was.

Now for sometime after this I remained predominately theocentric. But for the last two or three years and specially lately, more and more my whole religious life and experience seem centered with increasing vividness on our Lord—that sort of quasi-involuntary prayer which springs up of itself at odd moments is always now directed to Him. I seem to have to try as it were to live more and more towards Him only—it's all this which makes it so utterly heartbreaking when one is horrid. The New Testament, which once I couldn't make much of, or meditate on, now seems full of things never noticed—all gets more and *more* alive and compelling and beautiful. Sometimes the sense of His Presence is so vivid, I wonder what will happen next. And then of course come flat times when I wonder on the contrary if it was all a dream. Holy Communion, which at first I did simply under obedience, gets more and more wonderful too. It's in that world and atmosphere one lives. Now I feel rather uneasy about all this for:

(a) I know how fatally easy it is to slide into religious sentimentalism and make devotion into an emotional

satisfaction of a quite unspiritual kind and that
"consolations" have a very dangerous side. And I've a
*perfect* horror of all that sort of thing. Yet this is all so
calm and heavenly when it happens and so infinitely
beyond oneself and of course there are plenty of dull
and distracted times when one can only "carry on."
Perhaps it's only a Calvinistic twist that makes one
suspicious of yielding to such entrancing happiness, and
one ought to accept and be thankful. But in spite of the
reassuring things the books say, I do feel a sort of scruple
about it.

(b) The Baron used to say that a well-balanced religion
required the theocentric *and* incarnational sides
together: that no one got this quite right and most
fervent people were Christocentric to excess and let
their rightful devotion to our Lord swamp their sense of
God Himself, and the fact that not *even* Christ exhausted
the richness and possibility of God. He thought my
danger was in the opposite direction, but I don't know
what he would think now. Yet after all, St. Paul goes a
long way in the Christocentric direction, and it's the sort
of things he says, not all the horrible remarks of the Song
of Solomon-ish school of pietists, that now seem so
actual and so realistic.

(c) The increased concentration makes it so much
more difficult than before to meet on their own ground
the people who have arrived at a sort of all-overish
theism and feel "Hindus are often nearer God than
Christians," and that there are "other ways to Him" and
so forth. Certainly I do believe that He does reveal
Himself in many ways to those in good faith. But more
and more I do feel the *absolute* difference of real
Christianity, and it's this that these people won't admit.
At bottom Christ is to them an idea not a living fact and
that creates a barrier. It's the conviction of His
factualness that I'm powerless to give them—it doesn't
depend of course on argument—and anyhow I simply
*can't* speak about it. When they bring out all the stuff
about Christ being a world teacher, or the parallels of
the Mystery religions, the high quality of Buddhist

ethics, etc., I just feel what shallow, boring, unreal twaddle it is! But feeling that doesn't win souls for God—and it would be perfectly ghastly if one let oneself turn into a Pious Person comfortably ensconced in one's own prayers and with only one prescription to offer, wouldn't it?

3. This next winter I've had to say I'll do *no* lecturing, retreat work etc.—a disgusting concession to mere health which ought to be paid for somehow. So would it be all right, without making a rigid rule (for which I feel less and less need and inclination), to spend rather more time, when I can, in prayer and informal meditation? At present I am running my old rule of one and a half hours daily mostly in a very informal and take-it-as-it-comes sort of way. In my mixed and much interrupted life *exact* fixed times aren't possible.

This letter, probably written in late 1926 when Evelyn had put herself under the direction of Bishop Frere, is telling in a number of ways. The work of spiritual direction, which complemented her retreat work, was growing in its importance in her life. She was confused as to her own motivations in giving direction and fearful of using it as a means of power over others. Although the concern is legitimate, what is instructive is her sense of shame in discovering this possible motivation, and her response that "severe" measures must be taken against herself for this expression of self-will. This letter also shows her deepening commitment to Christocentric devotion. In chronicling her move from a theocentric to a Christocentric response, she notes her enormous debt to von Hügel. Her openness to the New Testament and her need for the Eucharist are both seen as part of her commitment to Christ as a living reality. Yet she continues to be fearful of these new commitments and worried that they might be expressions of religious sentimentality; and at the same time she chastises herself for her scruples, attributing them to a latent Calvinism in herself that might be suspicious of happiness.

Her Christocentrism presents problems for her interaction with others as well. She has obviously moved away from the theism of her earlier years, when she was herself absorbed with Tagore, to a position of the uniqueness of Christianity vis-à-vis other world religions. This must have been the beginning point of her reflection on this subject which would culminate in the publication in 1928 of "Christianity and the Claims of Other Religions," in which she asserts the uniqueness of Christian religion. The problem she confronts here is how to communicate the fact of Christ's living reality to others. It is not an argument to be made but a fact to be witnessed to.

Finally Evelyn alludes to her deteriorating health, a problem that will continue erratically until her death, forcing her from time to time to cut back on her work.

## Notes Made in Retreat, July 1927

1. I am asked for an absolute humble ungrudging forgiveness, to be renewed if necessary; recognizing that I am partly, even largely, to blame for what has happened and that my past faults and sins were patiently borne with, and my (at least virtual) disloyalties accepted. Also I must definitely exert myself to be more gentle, genial, and companionable, and to provide the relief and variety one needs and ought to get through home life. Mortify my own preference for quiet, carefully develope mutual interests, make up for any sacrifice made. And all this not out of prudence but out of charity; because it is part of the response asked by God.

2. I see that the sacramental life is and must be one with the crucified life. It is association with our Lord's whole sacrifice and incomplete without a share in the Cross. Must regard all suffering sent by God as an opportunity of this. The Eucharist marks the first station on the Way of the Cross.

3. If I could serve, humbly, generously, and lovingly, those who have in any way injured me, how great this would be.

4. Far more care and detailed love and devotion to the poor, and all the souls God sends me, without regard to personal preference.

5. Stern mortification of acquisitive and possessive

instincts—spend on others, give to others, demand
and expect *nothing*. Abandon all claimfulness and
grudging attitudes. Have a secret fear of discomfort
and poverty, which must go. *Choose* poverty and
neglect.

6. Carefully distinguish the two elements in my nature—
   steadily fight lower natural self-interested self—quietly
   and carefully feed spiritual self. "Self-love, self-will,
   and self-interest" still rampant in my soul even where
   disguised. Poverty of spirit is the only way out, with
   quiet letting-go of *all* rights and possessions and
   general support of rights and possessions of others.
   Not be distressed or afraid when things are taken from
   me: regard it as an honour.

7. Must more and more put the wine of religion into the
   water of common life; and try to appear less absorbed
   in purely religious interests, pick up and develope
   natural interests; especially those of other people.

8. More grateful recollection of all that has been given
   me: in love, friendship (e.g., Wilfred's devotion),
   saintly influences—the Bishop, Gwen, Rosa, etc.—
   utterly undeserved opportunities for work for God
   and encouraging results. Glad acceptance of failures,
   criticism, snubs, sense of isolation, when *those* come.

9. When people don't understand me, not to assume
   they are stupid or in the wrong.

10. Definite call to wide and generous spending of love—
    remember am minister of love, or *nothing*. Impossible
    to love *enough*. Especially try to include those to
    whom I'm not naturally attracted and who may be
    craving for love I ought to give: not the *à deux* kind
    but the entirely undemanding kind—the *gift*. Only if I
    give myself can I ever be consecrated.

11. Try to be more strict about my rule.

12. Am definitely committed to be a *disciple* of our
    Lord—be taught by Him, try to follow Him—and only
    as *this* does He give Himself to me sacramentally, as

one under discipline. Totally submitted, learning in
following, and at all costs including the Cross.

13. Realize I am a *very* slow learner and have only got on
a few inches yet, and my best experiences nothing at
all against what others have. In this retreat I have
been given finally a new and deeper state of prayer,
very interior and still, as if one was poured down
within oneself to an utterly hushed unmoving place
where one can remain, without apparent succession,
before Christ. Perhaps this is the "ground," bare and
silent.

14. Read the foregoing once a month till next retreat.

This retreat gives Evelyn a sense of well-being, but her notes are
again dominated by concern for her faults and her domestic responsibilities. She is being asked to forgive ungrudgingly, but she
acknowledges that she is in part to blame for some transgression.
She sees the need to develop more mutual interests, to mortify her
own preference for quiet, to be more companionable in order "to
get through home life." These references must relate to her relationship with Hubert who consistently remained uninterested in
her religious concerns.

She commends herself to "stern mortification" of possessive instincts and to "fight lower natural self-interests." She reminds herself to be grateful to Frere and her friends and to have a
wide-spreading inclusive love, a notion she borrowed from the
Flemish mystic Jan van Ruysbroeck.

## Notes made in Retreat, July 1928, Moreton

1. Review of the immediate past shows how little I have
carried out of what I understood in last retreat. Have
entirely forgotten to read my notes monthly. Have
fallen back into a morass of self-occupation,
claimfulness and irritability. Become enslaved by
undisciplined reveries, often tending to anti-Christian
and uncharitable day-dreaming and self-interested
brooding.

2. Tendency to tyranny, exactingness, getting my full
rights, etc., *must* be severely mortified. Considerate,
indulgent, conciliatory conduct best way of doing this.

3. Craving for human affection must be crushed; must give love freely and not examine the quality of what I get.

4. Lack of zest and love in dealing (a) with my poor (b) with cases; continued neglect of tiresome people, resentment about bothering and foolish correspondence. Forgetfulness of fact that God Himself comes to me in all these, and that it's an *honour* to be called on to serve them.

5. Am too authoritative and unwilling to do God's work in subjection to others, or in any way but what *I* like. Must be willing to accept all conditions and limitations (tiresome clergymen, sisters, etc.) and be humble and conciliatory, knowing how to yield in everything but essentials.

6. Chief need: steady practise of self-renunciation as to all work plans, tastes, affections, comforts, feelings, etc. Gradually submerge *all* personal desire in the ocean of Charity. Remember I am *not* my own property but His, and that I am utterly self-abandoned to His will and action, holding *nothing* back. Must be stricter and more mortified in small details of life. Check irritable comments and expressions of displeasure. Not indulge myself. Watch my ruling faults and temptations.

7. There is no place in my soul, no corner of my character, where God is not. Therefore there is no disposition, habit, or reaction to my environment, which can't be sanctified. I must give myself up to God's action far more completely than before, that he may actuate me wholly, since *I* am helpless.

8. I realise God does not and probably will not give me graces and lights for myself or my own consolation and advancement; but only that I may use them in His work. I am a *tool* and must accept this position. I shall never be adequate to the teaching He makes me impart. "The wind bloweth where it listeth" and blows through me for some mysterious reason, but

leaves my soul just what it was before. He has to use inferior souls—not enough of the others. I must be grateful, and not mind that my pupils do much better than I do.

9. My vocation is to a mixed life, and God comes to me, *not* only in prayer, etc., but in the opportunities of love and self-oblivion at home, at No. 3, with Clara, with cases and jobs, with the poor, in disregarding my own lassitude and aridity, and throughout all these varied frictions and opportunities preserving an interior spirit of tranquil joy and willingness to suffer when He wills. This seems almost impossible at present but at any rate must never permit myself to give it up as an ideal.

Beginning with these notes made at the retreat house at Moreton in 1928, the ferocity of Evelyn toward herself increases. The language is extremely harsh and self-condemnatory. She admits that she has needs for human affection and demands that they be filled, yet she simultaneously condemns herself for these needs that show that she is not abandoned to God. This "wound," as she later calls it, affects her relationship with others who appear to her more bothersome and irritating. This reaction causes her further reason for self-condemnation.

She sees her vocation as mixed, that is, not merely contemplative. Her work is in prayer and in loving Hubert, her parents who live at No. 3 Campden Hill Place, Clara Smith, who would accompany Evelyn and Hubert to Spain later that summer, and the poor that she has taken on in North Kensington. This is the ideal; but she admits she is far from balancing the active and contemplative life.

## Notes made in Retreat at Moreton, June 1929

1. Persistent failure in detachment and in escaping from the control of my own likes and dislikes. My inordinate longing to retain C.'s full affection and devotedness, and equally inordinate dislike of L.'s emotional clinging and dependence, sources of disturbance in my own inner life. To the question whether I could give C. up entirely, my whole nature

answers NO. So of first importance that this *attache* should be mortified and love purified. Must accept with *gratitude* each mark of coolness and indifference. Must be ready to yield as far as reason permits to L.'s demands and not show or harbour exasperation.

2. Futile to suppose I am called to or can develope a high type of prayer while I remain such an unstable pig. Don't really know *what* prayer I am called to. Only course is to respond gently and steadily to what is given, remembering Baron's warnings against all vehemence and strain.

3. Have ceased to make progress because I have refused to make sacrifices. Essential I should undertake deliberate renouncement (a) of my own comfort, which I always manage to secure; (b) of my preferences, social, personal, in work, etc.; (c) mortifying my repugnances under all above headings. Make a genuine effort to acquire a *genial indifference* as to what I do, who I meet, encourage, etc. Tiresome letters, cases, etc. My own plans, work, *not* to be clung to, or made reason for refusing help.

4. *Fraternal charity* the index of all real love of God. Don't love Him really until I love His manifestation in man, revere it, want to serve it, prostrate myself before it, ever see its merits and beauties. This means death to spirit of criticism, fastidiousness, coldness, lack of sympathy. On all these points *much* needs to be done. Constant watchful seizing of opportunities to serve, help, please, comfort others, not by role or as duty but in spirit of living love.

5. Should accept as form of suffering and humiliation cold Communion, persistent distractions and aridity and also the interior tempests I can't calm. Regard them as psychic illness, as to which one should take all possible measures and then bear what won't go, in submission to the cross of human nature laid on our souls.

6. Chief lights of this Retreat are *imperative* need of

active Detachment, Sacrifice, and Charity; the steady
cultivation and practice of Compassion, Sympathy,
self-oblivious kindness. *Do* Christian things however
humble and homely, not just believe them.

7. Nothing in my practical life can be a genuine reason
   for shirking the service of God, saying, "I cannot
   come." Must be ready to *act*, not always wait till
   pushed. *Do* the will more, not be just devotional, and
   do it in little humble loving ways. Great gentleness in
   all relationships. Never exacting. Never trying to get
   my rights. Definitely try to take lowest place, force
   myself to do it. Have been spoilt child. Now must
   genuinely grasp the Cross.

There is some indication that L. (Lucy Menzies) and C. (Clara
Smith), both directees of Evelyn and frequent participants in her
retreats, are rivals for Evelyn's affection. Although Evelyn considered Lucy a great friend, she sometimes found her irritating. At this
point Clara and Evelyn have some change in their relationship,
causing great agony for Evelyn, who speaks about having to give
up Clara entirely. As suggested, this may have to do with Clara's
conversion to Roman Catholicism, which probably occurred about
this time and would have necessitated an end to the relationship
with Evelyn as spiritual director. Evelyn is experiencing Clara's
coolness and indifference, which might make sense if in fact Clara
had "gone over to Rome" and would, given the demands of
Roman Catholicism at that time, necessitate terminating one's relationship with a non-Catholic spiritual director.

Evident is the ferocity of Evelyn's language toward herself.
Although she is under Frere's care, what helps her in her turmoil is
to recall von Hügel's advice warning against all vehemence and
strain.

## Father Talbot's Advice 1929-30[?]

1. As to the black fits: Lay out work more carefully to
   avoid overstrain and being constantly beset by people.
   Not *over* six retreats a year, plus spaces of quiet.

2. In times of peace deliberately concentrate on what is
   good and loveable in those who tend to upset me.

Take generous and indulgent view and reject hostile thoughts.

3. Be very wary about the things and people and conditions that make one specially accessible. Special care and control to do or think nothing in normal times to nourish or incite the other condition.

4. As to C., honestly recognize the relation has changed entirely; not let this rankle but have done with the past and accept gratefully from God what the present still gives. A certain distance may now have to be maintained and be the truest charity.

5. Apart from psychological and other causes, the spiritual meaning of these sufferings is vicarious, and they are, in so far as endured and not consented to, something I can offer to God and add to our Lord's cross as part of the battle with Evil.

6. The feeling of wickedness if not consented to is a temptation and so a form of suffering. It represents the eruption into consciousness of levels of one's nature which have to be left behind, discarded. Bear patiently what I can't overcome and offer it to God.

7. Panic enters into and increases this condition. To be met by prayer of confidence, "in thee have I trusted." It is like Bunyan's valley of Humiliation, when the pilgrim does not know whether the malicious voices he hears are his own.

These notes, copied probably in Marjorie Vernon's hand and without date, are contained in the flowered notebook but chronologically belong in the period 1929 to 1930. Talbot was a great admirer of von Hügel, and Evelyn may have sought his advice because of that connection.

There is every indication that Evelyn is overwrought, suffering, and in despair. She has been admonished to accept the fact that the relationship with Clara has changed, and that she should not give in to her sense of wickedness about it but offer all this to God.

### Bede Frost's Advice 1929-30[?]

To let the tumults happen as the way in which God is
purifying nature. Accept them and the obsession as
peacefully as I may, not struggle against them, but
exercise self-control; recognizing that my will is not in
this and that my comfort or discomfort don't in the least
matter. All that matters is the will of God, and this is just
my tribulation as much as was the thorn in the flesh of
St. Paul. So long as my will is Godwards it is all right.
Careful detachment from all inordinate affection for
creatures.

These notes, also from the flowered notebook, advise detachment. Von Hügel's advice was rather detachment within attachment, but Bede Frost advised a different emphasis.

## Notes made in Retreat, May 1930, St. Mary's Abbey, West Malling

1. Reviewing the past year, I see the spiritual blackness
   and agony of summer did do something for my
   growth as HWF [Howard Walter Frere] said. Prepared
   way for new kind of self-abandonment and a far
   deeper peace, felt during winter's illness, than ever
   before. Know too now I am able to do whatever God
   really wants me to do, *not* the things I want to do for
   Him. As towards God, progress ought to be along this
   path of active, confident self-abandonment; as
   towards others, continuous fight to reduce self-love
   and increase charity.

2. All the faults recognized in last retreat still rampant.
   Self-occupied, lacking in sympathy and gentleness,
   over sensitive, claimful, resentful, exacting in personal
   friendships. Easily bored and irritated, always
   forgetting to subordinate my own preferences and
   tastes. Slack, and unwilling to take trouble for others;
   no zest for cases or for the poor. Expect everyone to
   bear with me, while I don't bear with anyone
   properly.

3. In spite of all this, have experienced the power and help of God this year as never before (a) in delivering me from psychic and emotional storms (b) in filling me with strength to do a retreat when exhausted by illness (c) giving the interior knowledge of when I must accept helplessness, or when He wills me to make an effort in His service. If I am to retain these gifts it can only be through humbleness, simplicity and a great self-oblivion, all qualities I admire but haven't got.

4. Since it appears likely I will have indifferent health for the rest of my life, must face this quietly and gratefully, determine that it shall be the least possible worry and detriment to others, and fully used to purify and subordinate me to God's will. Steady effort to avoid dwelling on own physical state, getting into centre of picture, and accept the fatigue, weakness, monotony, dependence on others, nursing and humbling details of illness, with *joy.*

5. *No* real improvement in suppleness, general acceptance of interruptions, claims, tedious conversations, etc. This must be struggled for steadily.

6. God asks of me a determined war on self-love; a refusal both to be exactly myself and to resent or resist claims of others: check all irritations, claimfulness, fastidiousness, criticism and judging. Unlimited willingness to give; self-denial in time, interest, pity, affection, money. I have to remember that I neither am anything nor have anything save in Him. I am merely His tool.

7. Special war on hardness of all kinds and effort of charity to those I dislike and disapprove; look for beauty instead of faults in *all* souls I meet.

Evelyn claims that the agonizing summer of 1929 helped her grow in her abandonment to God, and that in spite of all her faults, which she continues to "fight" and make "war" on, she has experienced God's love in her psychic turmoil, in her illness and exhaustion, and in her growing self-knowledge.

## Lights from Retreat at 1932

1. Good thing to reduce journalism and odd jobs and accept loss of income as price paid for more spiritual leisure.

2. Two main lines of service—direct teaching, books, addresses, etc., and individuals. Space for both and neither to be pursued to point of exhaustion.

3. Much more careful nourishing of interior life.

4. Much more careful and general practice of charity.

5. Back again to steady religious drill.

6. I clearly see that suffering from depression, etc., however caused, can be transformed, purged of egotism and then offered with love and added to the Cross. I can then give thanks for the pain as constituting an acceptance of my self-offering and a phase in God's gracious work on my soul. This thanksgiving is very essential as I see it, for this acceptance and transformation of mental suffering uses and purifies both at once.

## Fruit of Retreat, 1933

1. A whole and complete self-offering to God for His unseen purpose, willing to accept suffering, darkness, struggle, temptation at His good pleasure.

2. A promise that wherever I go I will say Peace and try to bring Peace.

3. That I will give my own spiritual life without reserve into the keeping of God and strive to make my interior attitude one of weak adoration before God.

4. That I will seek to rejoice in the progress of others, especially those who overpass me, rejecting all movements of envy and spiritual jealousy, trying to take lowest place.

5. That I will be silent about my own interior sufferings and try to offer them to God.

*Tests.* Resist *every* inclination to say or suggest anything painful to C. Forget my rights. Accept for God all suffering under this head. Neglect no care, however tiresome. Be patient and loving with Rosa.

These two entries on the fruits of retreat are both found in the green notebook, but they are recorded in a different handwriting, probably that of Marjorie Vernon. They suggest some renewal of inner peace. It would be at about this time that she began to see Reginald Ward as a spiritual director.

## Easter Confession 1933, Reginald Somerset Ward

*As towards God.* Lack of generous, thorough joy, love, and so of unconditional surrender. Not living up in practice to my beliefs or promises. Knowing I must have suffering, make sacrifices and be purified, but afraid of what total transformation will cost and trying to dodge pain, and screaming and giving way to despair and bitterness when it really came. Letting myself feel hopeless and not giving priority to God's knowledge, love and penetration of me. Not being sufficiently grateful when He did heal me, still inclined to stroke the place and remember my troubles, not trusting Him to work in a way I don't like for the good of a soul I love, or freely abandoning what He has taken away.

Toying with the thought that the sense of God I sometimes have strongly is just imagination and doubting whether I really believe all I say when I am teaching. Sometimes a sort of dramatic faculty seizes me and I give an impression far beyond what I really live by or even see. When I notice this I feel an utter sham.

In general I have utterly failed to live my ordinary life in harmony with what God has shown me of Himself. Deep gap between action and prayer. Prayer itself fluctuating, distracted, self-regarding.

*As towards others.* I have sinned specially in regard to patience, gentleness and charity. Have avoided or failed in sympathy to those I find boring, have harboured critical and unkind thoughts and attitudes of mind. Have been guilty of explosions of irritation and hostile feelings towards tiresome neighbours and exasperation towards people who run after me and make demands when I don't want them, and write unnecessary letters. Instant movements of resentment if I suspect I am being deceived, managed or not openly dealt with. Impatience with the weakness of those who come for advice. Failure to remember the sacredness of my responsibilities.

I feel there is a horrible streak of hardness and bitterness somewhere in me, a resistance to the mortifying action of God through people which I've not eradicated and which keeps up a tension and conflict, and when touched up produces an awful hurly burly followed by utter exhaustion, and shows itself in rousing sharpness and unfair and intolerant judgements or— several times—in secret explosions of suppressed fury.

As towards my husband, I often fail to show interest in his affairs and amusements, not rousing myself to respond when I'm tired or concerned with other things; forgetting he is very patient with me and our difference in outlook must be just as trying for him.

In my relations with my father which are difficult and where I'm often met by coolness and indifference, I am constantly tempted to be cold and indifferent in my turn and feel it more and more difficult to be or feel loving or anything but a stranger. Yet I know that this too is a test if I could take it rightly.

In relations with friends, I am egoistic and governed by my preference for them rather than their needs. I always have time for those I am fond of and put off or forget those who do not attract. Neither to them nor to those I employ am I really longsuffering and kind or act towards them as representatives of God.

In this forthright confession to Ward found in the flowered note-book, Evelyn discusses her deepest suspicions about herself—her lack of trust, her possessiveness, her lack of belief, her inauthenticity. She speaks of a deep resentment, hardness, and bitterness, of sharpness and suppressed fury. In her closest relations with her husband, father, and friends she describes herself as basically un-interested, cool, indifferent, and egoistic. She never explores why she makes any of these responses, but rather only castigates her-self and turns all to God, of whom she never speaks as forgiving or having mercy on her.

## Reginald Somerset Ward's Advice, Holy Week 1933

Centre all effort on production and feeding of the gentleness of Christ, being His apprentice in the art of living and dealing with people, acting as He would act. Deliberately plan and carry through at least once a week the acting towards some person in His spirit of gentle-ness. This positive exercise is the best way of driving out hardness, sharpness, criticism and general uncharitable thought and behavior. No increase in prayer and very little self-examination. Three confessions yearly at most. To accept my vocation with simplicity and do my best, not encouraging scruples as to whether I'm good enough etc. Reduce tension and work where possible. Remember to give thanks for God's goodness. Be on guard against spirit of possession and clutch. Remember as regards work that I am simply a channel for Christ's action, but in myself a humble and sinful soul learning from Him. Keep these two aspects distinct.

Ward urges Evelyn to gentleness with others, thankfulness to God, and alertness against scruples, a disease characterized by a fixation on personal defects and an inordinate stress on the nega-tive. Ward believed that scruples was a form of "spiritual hypochondria," a self-centeredness that stifled prayer and inter-fered with the experience of God's love. Its origin was usually in severity toward a sensitive child and its cure lay in the stressing of God's love which diminished an "inflamed conscience," Ward urged Evelyn to focus on gentleness toward others, which would defeat her own pride, irritability, and anger.

## Reginald Somerset Ward's Advice, Michaelmas 1933

1. To tear down or get rid of the obsession as to my
   *general* badness, hopelessness and "divided nature,"
   etc., which is not true humility but defeatism.
   Acknowledge and make war on *specific* sinful
   dispositions, thoughts and acts, but drop depressed
   attitude toward my nature in general and think rather
   of God's grace and all He has done for me. Best not to
   think in terms of dissociation and shelter behind it,
   but regard myself as one, for the whole of which I am
   responsible to God.

2. Careful distinction between temptation and sin. The
   arising of angry and uncharitable thoughts *never*
   enough for sin. Only the consent of the will involves
   sin. Refuse and reject first thought always—if it insists
   on staying, even the struggle with it may still not
   involve sin. The temptation itself contains material of
   mortification which, if rightly used, can become
   something to offer to God.

3. As regards present trouble, the suffering, etc. are the
   result of pride as well as possessiveness. Humbly
   accepting the situation in its wholeness, going out of
   one's way to be nice about it, deliberately refusing
   opportunities of sharp, clever criticism and—when
   thought of—not uttering them, and taking these
   renunciations to Communion and offering them to
   God as done for Him will extract real gold from the
   situation.

4. Remember I have a very delicately balanced psycho-
   physical nature which it is my duty to keep in good
   working order for God. Moderation, variety, care
   about day off and non-religious interests. Bodily
   austerities not really practicable at my age; but
   mortification of thought and speech, patience,
   gentleness to take its place, especially deliberate
   renunciation of criticism, etc. Some mild abstinence,
   etc., possible but *not* to be binding, or its omission
   regarded as sin.

5. Great freedom in prayer. Rule of life to be abolished. Follow God's leading, avoid strain, no sense of sin when my usual times are not kept. The simple childlike gazing and immersion is the real thing. Avoid self-occupation and dwelling on faults, etc.

6. Prayer after Communion. The Blood of Christ permeates every atom of my being; may the Father see me as beautiful, being robed in His Beauty.

The second part of Ward's program was to convince Evelyn to reject her defeatism and general negativism about herself and to see herself "as beautiful, being robed in His Beauty." In short, he was trying to have her focus on the fact that she was loved by God, something which, at least in these notes, she never mentions.

## Reginald Somerset Ward's Advice: Later

The root trouble is intense possessiveness, deeply and suddenly injured and unable to adapt itself. The result is the formation of a severe neurosis, having a deep scar right across the soul. Condition is aggravated by chronic overstrain. But the Godward life is still active and still strongest. *Treatment:* avoid touching or rousing the wound still too tender to bear it. Leave that, accepting the fact that the bouts of suffering do arise from the above cause. But seek every occasion of mortifying possessiveness and claimfulness in small things. Relax grip and clutch. Attack the whole tendency in detail. Avoid all strain.

Ward sees the immediate cause of Evelyn's "trouble" as possessiveness which has resulted in "severe neurosis." There is no indication here that he explored the psychological reasons for this, although certainly in his *Guide for Spiritual Directors* he indicates that most spiritual maladies have their origin in fear in its various forms, which blocks close contact with God and hence weakens trust. Fear was usually rooted in one's early life, was generally repressed during youth and adolescence and emerged again as one matured. As he saw it, the goal of the spiritual director was to help a person discover the fear that dominated his or her life.

Persistent in Underhill's life is an unforgiving harshness toward herself, which must have contributed both to her irritability and her longing for intimacy and acceptance, which she translated as possessiveness. Ironically, the woman who could speak and write so eloquently of the love of God as she saw it in the lives of others could not experience it consistently in her own life.

## Reginald Somerset Ward, January 1934

1. The obsession is gradually dying and keeping it under lock and key will help its extinction. Not to worry over gusts of resentment, etc., as these are more results of the old wound than real sinful unforgivingness. Continue to offer all suffering and acts of resignation, self-conquest, etc., to God.

2. *Not* to allow myself to use prayer and what comes in it for my work; note lights received in meditation, but consider . . . to any recollection, giving the time wholly to God. Most important thing.

3. Remember, the element in prayer that matters is desire not satisfaction. Everything offered to God with the desire to worship Him counts, and may be a far better prayer than spells of contemplative happiness. So persevere in acts, however apparently unrewarding.

4. Distracted condition largely arises from strain and points to more entirely non-religious recreation and leisureliness.

5. Remember the whole of God's undivided love is poured out on my soul and is the *cause* of my personality as well as my power of response. To think more of this than of my love for Him and open my soul to it.

There is a glimmer here of the end of self-preoccupation. The subject here is prayer as worship and the importance of desire as the essence of prayer.

Point five is particularly noteworthy. Here she remembers that Ward spoke of God's undivided love for her. Her focus should not be on her love for God, which will always be imperfect, but on God's love for her. She is to open her soul to this love.

## Fruits of Retreat 1934

- A determination to deepen and widen charity, to check all unloving thoughts, criticisms, words, etc.

- War on slightest movements of anger, jealousy and pride.

- Remember that only the life of charity *can* unite to God, the all-loving will.

- Surrender my life and desires again and again to Him and seek for active expressions of love, especially to those where it is difficult.

- Patience, geniality, never refusing myself, never bored.

- Mix charity and work well up with contemplative prayer.

- Complete suppleness in God's hand: to suffer or not to suffer, work or not work: abandon and industry together. Give up all clinging to my influence, etc. Be willing and ready to decrease.

## Reginald Somerset Ward, June 19, 1934

1. Be honest with God and not blame myself for what as a matter of fact I can't help, e.g., distractions, temptations and uncharitable thoughts.

2. In dealing with distractions, directly I perceive them *at once* take a book, use collect, write down aspiration and so on.

3. Avoid confession—once a year only—encourages subjectivism.

4. Most careful discrimination of temptation from sin. A resisted temptation is an offering one can make to God.

5. My way should be that of dependence and abandonment. No more struggle to be what I think I'd like to be, but a total yielding of myself to God. Not standing about on brink saying I'm not good enough, but a plunge into the sea without *retour sur soi- même.*

6. In prayer, however distracted, the actual time set apart for God, even if apparently wasted, is something offered to Him. So one must try to see it out, though it may seem all spent in wandering and unworthy thoughts.

7. As regards others: (a) Persist in affectionate attention to F[ather], however cool the response. (b) Take great pains to be actively sympathetic with H[ubert]'s interests. (c) Never yield to the temptation to tick W[ilfred] off when she tries to give me religious information. And offer all three forms of mortification to God.

8. Health. Decide an amount of rest and care really needed. Do this as a duty and leave the rest in God's hands.

Ward urges her not to blame herself, not to feed her sense of guilt in confession, and not to berate herself about unfocused prayer. As regards domestic relationships he suggests affectionate attention, sympathy, and patience.

## Retreat, 1935

- No shirking of distasteful jobs, people, situations, etc., and other efforts to serve God against the collar. Letters to unattractive cases first.

- No expressions of vexation, contempt, hardness, criticism, etc., of those I don't care about. No preference to things I do like—M[argaret Cropper] for instance.

- No oblique vengeance on W[ilfred] and R[oman] C[atholic] Church in any way.

- No indulgence of boredom. No seeking excuses for my own way, prejudices and so on.

- Resist inclinations of nature; turn wholly to my worship of God; seek the inspiration of Grace.

Evelyn's retreat summaries for 1934 and 1935 both reflect that, although Ward urges her to gentleness toward others and an appreciation of God's love for her, she continues to fix on her faults and failures. She seems to ignore Ward's admonition that she focus on God's love for her rather than her love or lack of love for God.

## Notes for Reginald Somerset Ward, October 1936

1. D. Swayne's address

2. Am not in the least reluctant to draw in and give up expressive work, but so far don't make anything of it. If God really *means* me for a waterpipe, then putting the cork in will throw things out of gear. At first I felt sure—now I feel unsure. Don't get any prayer done. Feel reluctant to do retreats but this may be just the effort. Have lost interest in this sort of work, but that doesn't prove I oughtn't to do it!

3. What about Rule? Communion? A Quiet Day a month? Whole life needs more careful organizing.

4. Faults, nerves, irritability, Rosa's death, H.

5. Personal relations—L. M.

**Virtues of Christ**

Patience. Forgiveness. Humility. Entire abandonment to God. Gentle consideration of others. Acceptance of hardships.

I think mortification of the senses takes on a new importance now and is essential to recollection. Custody of the eyes and the tongue. Some *hints* for these? Examples of bodily discipline in normal life.

Attention wanders about—too mercurial. Easily led off into lively conversation, uncharitable tales and

comments; amusing criticisms. All this seems more and
more hostile to prayer. Thick layer of cotton wool
between my soul and God.

She has a number of questions to address to Ward. The faults
are there, as are the questions over relationships with Lucy
Menzies and Hubert. She is considering giving up some of her
work. This consideration arises after two years of labor on *Worship*
which placed an enormous burden on her. Here she refers to the
waterpipe image of Teresa of Avila. If one is a waterpipe through
which God's love flows, is it right to cork it up? In short, should
she cease writing, giving retreats and so forth? She is unsure.

## Quiet Day, Feb. 4th [1937?]

1. Strip off all—give all—don't make a profit out of
   religious work. No limit to God's demand.

2. Gone badly wrong in making money profit out of
   broadcasts—turned respectable girl into prostitute;
   punished directly by its humiliating appearance.
   Whole thing wrong. Mustn't keep the extra money,
   owe fifteen pounds to the Lord. No more trying for
   the highest terms—God and Mammon. Work to be
   laid on the altar and left there.

3. Dying to the world, buried with Christ become more
   drastic and thorough as one goes on. Must *be* buried
   to be raised by God's Glory.

4. More sustained and serious effort to be interested
   companion to H[ubert] and make his home
   comfortable and happy.

In late 1936 Underhill prepared a series of radio broadcasts for
the BBC on the spiritual life. She apparently accepted payment for
this and here expresses her guilt about this. Again, she urges herself to be more attentive to Hubert and to make him happy.
Although there is every indication that she and Hubert respected
each other, they apparently had little in common, although they
shared recreational time together.

## Notes in Retreat, [1937?]

No love without pain. Now am better than I have been for two years and *physically* quite capable of retreats, etc. Entirely a spiritual question as to whether I should do them. *Prioress* says: keep out of all the traffic of the world for the present—very important. But this would involve not mixing with people as well as not doing jobs. When I can shut off the world—quiet days or so on—I do live at a wholly different level and gradually get into another state and attitude. But I can't keep this up in the ordinary way. So far I have nothing at all to show for reduced work and engagements except improved nervous and general health, which was *not* my object.

Mixing with theologians, etc., *does* excite and distract and give me pleasure.

On the other hand, I do know the *right path* is poverty and self-stripping. Yet I've been given, as a matter of fact and without demanding or trying for it, rather more success than usual lately. Is this just temptation or God's will?

*Prayer*—either utterly distracted or else silent absorption in God. These late Communions very miserable business, but will have to go on till winter ends. By the time one gets to church already distracted for the day. *Dispositions*—much too hard-hearted. I notice real people of prayer made acutely unhappy by suffering or evil, but it *never seems* to take me like that. Can't concentrate my mind on it. Though I may be rather distressed on the surface, or worried, impatient, etc., a sort of fundamental calm never disturbed, which may be and probably is, just callousness and want of love.

*Ruling.* All right—not my type to be afflicted. Damp everything down even if formal. Pray about the common place things of daily life.

Illness had given Evelyn some rest and hence peace, and *Worship* had given her success, a broader subject, and wider audi-

ence. This produced renewed pleasure. Although she appreciates
this, she is somewhat detached, knowing her real inner work is
what is needed. She continues to be suspicious of her own re-
sponsiveness, in this case her inability to be made unhappy by evil
or suffering. While she takes the advice of the Carmelite prioress
seriously, she returns to her commitment to stay in the world for
its sake: this has been her vocation for decades.

## Fruit of Retreat [1937?]

New sense of penetrating presence and action of God
and my own subjugation. Immense need of purification
of will, stopping self-chosen work and self-satisfying
work. Humbled under mighty hand of God.

Determined use of every opportunity to improve in
gentleness, to take real trouble about uninteresting
people, to be accessible and responsive.

Elimination of hardness and curb judgements: more
generosity, less criticism. Check on grumbling. Welcome
of vexations and contradictions as scraps to offer to God.
Real effort toward recollection. Early prayer, not just
doze among pillows. Mass twice weekly with self-
offering to God. Also, the points of discipline already
noted.

In these final notes, probably from mid-1937, Evelyn both senses
the presence of God and sees the need to let go of her work,
which had for years given her life meaning. This was what she
called "the laying down of tools." Lecturing and retreats ended,
and writing was kept to a minimum.

# AFTERWORDS

After Evelyn Underhill's death Lucy Menzies, her friend of many years, was surprised when she came across these notebooks. She had known Evelyn throughout this entire period and had no sense of her inner turmoil. Apparently Evelyn shared this aspect of her life with no one other than her directors. While she conducted retreats, gave spiritual direction, and wrote, she also chronicled her doubts, her failings, and her experiences of God's presence. *Fragments From an Inner Life* opens up her life, illustrating both her joys and sorrows, and giving credence to the belief that the work of the spirit continues, even into this century.

# APPENDICES

The following three reports were written by Evelyn Underhill to Baron von Hügel during the period 1921 to 1923. Although not part of her notebooks, they provide background material for understanding them. The first and second reports were written prior to the green notebook. The third, written at the end of June 1923, indicated that she used the notebook as a device for recording ideas and experiences she wanted to share with von Hügel. The originals of these reports are not extant; typescripts are in the archives of the University of St. Andrews, Scotland, transcribed by Lucy Menzies, Underhill's first literary executrix.

# APPENDIX I

## December 21, 1921

The chief point is, am I simply living on illusion? It seems impossible but all the same, I feel I must be sure. I don't mean by any unwillingness to make a venture or any demand for impossible clearness of faith, but simply to be *certain* my own experiences are not simply imaginary. The points in favour of their reality seem to be (a) what you call *given-ness*; unexpectedness, entire non-earnedness (b) overwhelming sense of certitude, objective reality and of obligation (c) that I have never tried either to obtain or retain them, and know any such effort would be useless. I leave out the merely emotional side as that is said to be no guarantee of genuineness. All the same it is difficult to conceive that a construction of one's mind could produce such feeling. I have had this sort of experience on and off for over sixteen years, since a sort of conversion experience of a quite definite sort which put a final end to a (very uncomfortable) period of agnosticism. This had happened before you first knew me, and I then very nearly became a Catholic but didn't quite. However, I went on for a long time going to Mass on Sundays as a sort of freelance and outsider; but gradually this faded out in favour of what I vainly imagined to be *inwardness*, and an increasing anti-institutional bias. Then, during the war, I went to pieces as I told you: though with several vivid calls-back which I did not respond to. Now I have got back, but what seems to me so strange and makes me nervous is that I should have expected to have to fight my way back inch by inch. Instead of that everything has been given back to me that I ever had, and more. I can't go into this, but I do just want to know whether such a completely undeserved restitution is normal and all right, and whether the process of behaving like a rebellious, hardened and contracted beast—mind getting into utter blackness—then realizing it, however bitterly, can be an actual way of development. Is this sort of experience what is meant by *forgiveness*? Because that is what it felt like—final and complete, reharmonizing and secure.

Of course I know all the arguments and could explain it all quite nearly to myself on psychological lines; but that sort of thing seems very unreal when you are faced by reality and does not allow for the strange sense of being personally dealt with, which must, I suppose, be in part illusion?

Of course the door will shut again, is indeed shut now, but that does not so particularly matter. So the first point is: Is all the above real? and can I trust it? or am I living by a dream? If the answer is favourable—am I still obsessed by "pure mysticism"?

What ought I to do? I am having too easy a time and ought to do something hard—some modern equivalent of a hair-shirt that would keep on reminding one. And being naturally self-indulgent and at present unfortunately professionally very prosperous and petted, nothing will get done unless I make a Rule. Neither intellectual work nor religion give me any real discipline because I have a strong natural attraction to both. So anything practical you will tell me about that will be a great help. But it is useless advising anything that people could notice or that would look pious. That is beyond me. In my lucid moments I see only too clearly that the only possible end of this road is complete unconditional self-consecration and for this I have not the nerve, the character, or the depth. There has been some sort of mistake. My soul is too small for it and yet it is the only thing at bottom that I really want. It feels sometimes as if, whilst still a jumble of conflicting impulses and violent faults, I were being pushed from behind towards an edge I *dare not* jump over.

In your second letter you emphasized that whatever one's rule about institutionalism it should be constant, not added to much in time of light or reduced in times of darkness. Does this apply all round? e.g., should there be an average rule about times given to prayer, etc.? Not to add or reduce this? That seems fearfully difficult. It seems such mere waste of time when you are shut off, to say over verbal prayers that have no meaning for one, and perpetually try to capture a wandering attention; five minutes then seem like an hour. And it seems equally hard saying that one may not add on time, when one has a strong impulse to and can manage it without neglecting necessary work.

However, if you will say what I ought to do about this, I shall try to do it. My tendency has been to very wide variations; scamping everything in dark times, which in these last years have of course been pretty constant: and anyhow I don't give a great deal of definitely set-apart time—not more than one hour a day as a rule and often less. Probably I ought to try and make time to increase this.

Christocentric devotion. This is still a difficulty. I can't do it. And yet the average Christian appears by declaration to do it naturally and instinctively. It seems to me to involve the fusion of two incompatible conceptions. Yet I really *am* a Christian—at least I believe so—though in the modernist rather than a strict orthodox sense. But God seems to me the centre and the only inevitable Object of adoration and, anyhow, all that I know at first hand. *Is* this all right? It is very far from the negative, unconditioned sort of apprehension which I understand is what you condemn, but is on the contrary more coloured, vivid, real, and personal than anything else. But *not* human.

# APPENDIX II

## Mid-summer 1922

1. *Invisible religion.* Inwardly, till the last few weeks, I have had rather a rough time. When I came to you, I was frantic and feverish, and afterwards that was worse and got altogether too near the psycho-physical danger zone. I had to stop it, with resulting dimness, great restlessness and not knowing what to be at. Then, by the beginning of Lent, I got into a state of vague increasing inward suffering and struggle, as if one were fighting shadows and more and more obsessed by *the feeling of sin.* I could not think of anything else and lost my spiritual world-view. It was just as if one's soul were being scorched. Useless to tell myself I had got to practise self-oblivion— impossible to forget it except when with my poor people. I was beginning to be faintly Christian then, but it spoilt my Communions and I dreaded times of prayer—they meant dimness, incapacity, pain and *horrible remorse.*

By Holy Week I was so tortured, I decided to go and make a general confession (1) because I had always loathed the idea, so it would be something definite to do, and (2) I thought perhaps it would be like a spring cleaning; I would be all right afterwards. Probably I ought not to have done it without your permission, but felt I must.

It was not a bit like a spring cleaning and I did not feel a scrap absolved; but as a humiliation it left absolutely nothing to be desired. It is one thing to make voluntary

acts of abjection to God and quite another when a
human being forces you to realize your own utter
beastliness. You were much too kind to do this; but the
man I went to devoted his time to smashing me up.
When he had finished, I felt utterly degraded, hopeless,
and smirched all over. The very next day I found two
horrible insects kissing one of my little slum children. Of
course you will laugh at this or feel I should not bother
you with such trifles. But the point is, on the top of all
the rest, it seemed to complete the ruin of my self-
respect and filled me up with horror and self-loathing. I
felt vile through and through, body and soul—just
rubbed in the mud.

And the queer thing is, it was then—when I could not
look at or think of transcendent holiness—that I realized
what the agonizing need is that only Christianity *can*
meet, by coming right down to one in the dust. *St.
Augustine was a thousand times right!* Plotinus can
never have had to face his own beastliness. Neo-
Platonism goes to bits when one gets really to the
bottom and knows oneself unmendably displeasing to
God.

I stayed at the bottom for weeks with occasional
moments of peace but mostly suffocated by the
unescapable sense of sin and utter rottenness. I confess I
had times of blackest depression and fed-upness, when it
seemed the strain could not be borne, or the utter
loneliness. Religion seemed suddenly to have become
savage and unrelenting. Gradually it wore off a bit and I
crept out, but miserably conscious I should never be any
good.

Then, at Ascensiontide, I went into retreat at Pleshey.
This was not another case of taking the law into my own
hands—the Warden is a friend of mine and I had
promised to go before you took charge of me. I went
with a lot of elementary school teachers from the East
End. It helped me a great deal. The intense silence
seemed to slow down one's far too quick mental time
and give one's soul a chance. To my surprise a regime of

daily Communion and four services a day with silence between, was the most easy, unstrained and natural life I had ever lived. One sank down into it, and doing it always with the same people, all meaning it intensely, and the general atmosphere of deep devotion—for the whole house seems soaked in love and prayer—cured solitude and gave me at last really the feeling of belonging to the Christian family and not counting except as that. I lost there my last bit of separateness and wish for anything of my own and gained a wholly new sense of the realness and almost unbearable beauty of the Christian life. I came away quite tranquil and determined on the entire surrender and so far have not wavered from that—though again and again I have fallen far below it and done and said things inconsistent with it. Anyhow I know now what I ought to be like, if my love were of better quality.

The *general result* of these adventures, as far as one can make them out, is: I have lost the violent and overwhelming sort of consciousness I had six months ago; and also lost, alas! (for many months now) the prayer of quiet—which seems a real set-back. But I have a sort of dimmer but on the whole, steadier sense; varying a good deal in character and intensity and often only a vague background feeling, but seldom past recall, though there *are* utterly blank days. Much gentler than it was and yet more penetrating and spreading in a way.

My old religious life now looks too thin and solitary: this is more various—contemplation, Holy Communion, the felt presence of God, struggles to behave properly, and love for my poor people—all seem articulated points of it. All sense of contact departs abruptly the minute I become critical or horrid or fail in love and patience, or otherwise fall below my none-too-high standard.

As to practices: what help and feed me most are Holy Communion and short, constant bits of recollection and prayer (when I am not too rushed to remember them). The Retreat was like a week on the glaciers—bracing, purifying, and calming. *I should like to do this several*

*times a year—it would be time well spent.* On the other
hand, I think regular confession would wreck me
altogether. It tears me to bits, leaves me in a state of
nervous illness and encourages my hateful and
unconquerable habit of introspection. Apart from Holy
Communion, I cannot honestly say church-going attracts
me much and I seldom go to Benediction now. Silent
prayers seem as easy and fruitful at home as in church.

2. *Visiting the Poor.* This prescription has been a
complete success. I realize now I was starving for
something of that kind. It is an immense source of
interest, often of a heart-breaking kind; for they are
always in some sort of trouble or misery, poor
darlings—often actually hungry—and it is so little one
can do to rescue them. I got eight families from a
friend who had wrecked her health by devoted work
for them and others, and as they adored her, I come in
quite second best (though all are good friends with
me) so there is no food for vanity! On the contrary,
one comes away feeling an utter worm; comparing
one's own secure life with their incessant struggles
and anxieties and the amazing courage and sweetness
with which they bear it. The women are perfectly
wonderful. If I were like my particular friend, living in
a basement with six restless children, poor health,
endless difficulties and a drunken cruel beast of a man
to whom she is not even married, I should go
completely to bits. It all makes one feel, religiously as
well as physically, rather pampered. I think more and
more, unless one can stretch out one's own
devotional life to make it avail for them ( for they have
not any and how *can* they have), it remains more or
less a spiritual luxury. But I do not see how to do this
in any real way at present. Nor, except getting one
baby christened, have I yet found any outlet for
religion. It is mostly a case of being a family friend and
general cheerer-up—not at all a spiritual job! Of
course sometimes it is taxing and a bit of an effort,
but on the whole a source of real happiness, not
mortification, so the screw will have to be put on

somewhere else. The queer thing is the tranquillizing effect they have. However jangled one may be when one goes to them, one always comes away mysteriously filled with peace and nearer God.

You were absolutely right: they give one far more than one can ever give them, and I feel I ought to give them *much* greater love and compassion then I do. Of course the temptation is to concentrate on the most attractive but I try not to do that. I am afraid a good deal of time is spent simply consorting with the little kiddies and feeding them with chocolate. This is not a very elevated occupation I know, but it means a lot to me. You see, when you have none of your own, it does rather freeze you up; and I am too shy and awkward to get on with educated kids. But these are such nice and friendly appealing little creatures, like tiny flowers in those grimy places; and one can enjoy them without self-consciousness or anyone knowing. I can't tell you what a sense of expansion and liberation I have got from this.

3. *Direction work.* I have not had much to do in this, except keeping one or two old cases going, but am now doing more than before in the way of instructions, addresses to Guilds, collections of clergymen, etc. And I think I had better take all this sort of work that offers as it is direct and inconspicuous and seems really to be needed.

4. *Detachment and general behaviour.*

(a) Really because I have been so absorbed in religious interests and struggles, I have not felt the old temptations to exactingness, jealousy, etc., in personal relations, but expect this is only dozing, not killed. I still find people attractive, but can now take friendships rather less intensely. All the same, in many ways I am still absurdly over-sensitive and easily tipped off my spiritual balance by worries and vexations, though I do stamp down this sort of thing and refuse to luxuriate in it, and so scramble back rather more quickly than before. It is a struggle to leave *all* one's

professional vanity at the foot of the Cross—but
unless I can do this, I may as well give up
altogether.

(b) Even although I manage to stifle a good bit of my
boundless impatience, capacity for exasperation,
and snappy temper (formerly written off as due to
nerves and over-work), still, some pops out if I am
off my guard and the rest seethes inside for a bit.
All the same, one *can* win these battle's if one
does not shirk them, if not at the moment, at least
next day.

(c) All the strains and conflicts come in with ordinary
active life: professional and social intercourse,
family duties, perpetual scrimmage to adjust rival
claims and fit everything in, opportunities of
accepting boring things, etc. Here I don't think I
improve. I pick out objects of devotedness instead
of taking obvious and unattractive ones. Though
except when nervous and cross, I do find people
in general far more loveable and feel more tolerant
and less critical towards them; still, I fail perpetually in gentleness, love and abnegation. One trues
oneself up on Sunday, but it peters out very soon.

(d) I am also very cowardly ( I like to call it reserve)
about my mostly pagan friends and entirely non-
church-going family suspecting how much I care
for religion, and descend to almost any evasions
and concealments to avoid this. I live in a nervous
terror of discovery, make elaborate plans to get to
Holy Communion unobserved and let my rule
pass when staying with people, rather than seem
pious. This is despicable from one point of view;
but all the same there is a horribleness in letting
one's treasures be seen.

(e) As for eternal oblivion, it seems *hopeless.*
Incessant introspection and eternal self-
communings seem to possess me: I hate it but
can't get away from it. It ruins my prayers very
often and is, I know, altogether wrong. Now and
then one gets away from it and all tangles, into the
depths and is nothing—but this is very seldom
and only for a bit.

5. *Prayer.*

(a) You told me to practise the kind and degree that "most humbled yet braced." But I can't stick to one kind or degree: I range from complete self-absorption, or mixed silence and aspirations (which I think is the kind that suits me best really), to mere chatterings, vague considerations and wandering attention. Orderly Three Point Meditations seem impossible and a good deal of the (very short!) time you allowed is wasted in distractions. I wish I could have a bit more latitude about this. You see, if one has to scurry round one's house, order meals, etc., just before, it does not put one in the most favourable state for recollection; and often most of that half hour is spent trying to get recollected. On the other hand, when the states of real absorption which alone are really worthwhile happen, they take time to get established, and then the time is up and I have to break off forcibly. I have really been very obedient about this but *would* like to feel freer and would not, I promise, make it an excuse for religious daydreaming. I would like a minimum of one hour and a maximum of one and a half hours; to include morning and night prayers, but not odd five minutes during the day. Also, when I can't get to the Carmelites in the afternoon, or only at the price of over-fatigue, to take that quarter of an hour at home instead.

(b) I feel I ought to spend more time in intercession and would if I could feel it did real work. But it is so unreal to me that I forget all about it. Yet I know that when you pray for me, you do somehow bring a tremendous force to bear! And even in my tiny way I ought to be able to do something, especially for the souls I have got to try to help. In general I forget all specific requests—after all, why *should* one ask for things? To bring one's deepest desires and intentions and moral difficulties into the Presence of God and hold them there is of course tremendously effective, but trying to affect other people's lives in this way seems to me at present to belong more

to the realm of idea than to that of concrete fact. I
am almost certainly wrong about this and blinded
here as I was in other directions and I want to get
it right, because I must give my devotional life
*some* redemptive and social character and prevent
it getting too thin and vertical.

(c) You said further, my aim must be to keep as
continuously as possible in the spirit of prayer.
Well, I made an awful struggle for this, but if by it
you mean *conscious* constant tendency and
aspiration to God, it is beyond me. When working
it splits my attention hopelessly; and when with
other people it vanishes. Although there are
whole days, especially in the country when I am
much alone, I can do it, there are more when I
forget for hours. If, however, you mean only a sort
of dim background awareness, a vertical
orientation to God, and now and then short and
very simple recollection for a minute or two, I can
more or less do this. But it is too easy and too
superficial to be what you really mean, I feel sure.

6. *Christocentric devotion.* I take back, with shame,
every word I said against this. This does not, however,
mean a devotional *volte-face.* I am still mainly
theocentric; but the two attitudes are no longer in
opposition in my mind—they are two aspects of one
thing. Something you said showed me how to bridge
the gap between theism and Christian devotion,
which had worried me for years and lately had been
driving me steadily in a direction not *much* removed
from Unitarianism, as you perceived (though I did not
at all like it when you said so!). Now I have got my
universe all in one piece again. This has meant
throwing overboard some Nicene language about pre-
existence, eternal generation, etc., and Platonic
conceptions of the Logos-Christ. But perhaps you will
allow a little latitude here.

7. *Historical values in religion.* Yes! I now fully and
solidly accept your position, with no reserves at all;
and with a growing feeling in favour of such historical
realism and dislike of fluffy and notional instead of

factual religion. You forced me thoroughly to reconsider my own foundations and realize that a mere philosophy of value, however sublime, has no power to redeem unless these values have been incarnated in human life. The main historical happenings as given by reasonable New Testament criticism—e.g. and especially the Passion—are absolutely necessary to Christianity as I understand it. I never doubted their occurrence, but they now mean a great deal more to me. Also as regards to Holy Communion, the historical link comes in strongly and at least part of what it means to me (putting aside the purely spiritual and quite undiscussable aspect) is the feeling of being linked with, and doing, the same thing as all the others who have really cared, right from the beginning—and through them stretching back to the beginning too. A sort of spiritual time-stream. You may say as a non-Catholic, I do nothing of the kind, but I do not think you *will*; anyhow, that is how I feel it.

8. This is really a continuation and development of the preceding. I feel I do not yet fully understand all you said under this head, but sometimes for a bit I do. Anyhow I fully accept and trust it.

9. *Spiritual dispositions.* Here again, while fully accepting what you say, I have only been able very partially to practise it. The transcendental and incarnational currents *are* woven together now and there is not opposition between them in my mind. But the incarnational current is still the weakest. If my soul is left to itself, it moves off in the non-spatial, theocentric direction at once. I do try by persistent New Testament reading and meditation to strengthen the strictly Christian side and it is never quite out of my mind—but the other is most vividly and factually present.

10. I accept this theory, though whether I am yet equal to performing it in practise is more doubtful. Frankly I cannot at present conceive the question of sub-

mission to Rome, as to which this point first came up, ever becoming a case of conscience. In fact, I feel now quite satisfied as an Anglican, having discovered a corner I can fit into and people with whom I can sympathize and work. Still, it *might* happen, and if it did, I *hope* I should not draw back.

# APPENDIX III

## June 1923

1. *General.* I feel quite different from last year; but in ways rather hard to define. Deeper-in. More steady on my knees though not yet very steady on my *feet.* Not so rushing up and down between blankness and vehement consolations. Still much oscillation, but a kind of steady line persists instead of /\/\/\/\.

Been trying all the time to shift the focus from feeling to will but have not fully done it, and shall not feel safe till I have.

The Christocentric side has become so much deeper and stronger—it nearly predominates. I never dreamed it was like this. It is just beginning now to dawn on me what the Sacramental Life really does involve: but it is only in flashes of a miraculous penetration I can realize this. On the whole, in spite of blanks, times of wretched incapacity and worse (see below), I have never known before such deep and real happiness, such a sense of at last having got my real permanent life and being able to love without stint where I am meant to love. It is as if one were suddenly liberated and able to expand all round. Such joy that it sometimes almost hurts. All this, humanly speaking, I owe entirely to you. Gratitude is a poor, dry word for what I feel about it. I can't say anything.

2. The moral struggle is incessant but there is a queer joy in it. I don't think I need bother you much about that. Small renunciations *are* easier, but real ones still

mean a fight. Nervous tension or exhaustion means a
renewed attack of all my old temptations at full
strength and I feel invaded by hard, exasperated,
critical, hostile, gloomy and unloving inclinations.

Of course my *will* does not consent to these horrors: I
do struggle with them; all the same they creep into my
mind and stick for days—another proof that at bottom
I'm unchristian still; for surely mere nervous tension
should not mean these odious feelings? And that lovely,
gentle suppleness and radiance I see in all my real
Christian friends, and long for, I can't get. I don't think I
have yet ever seen the deepest roots in myself of pride
and self-love.

Many religious practices I still can't do, e.g., self-
examination. I did make myself do a long written one at
my retreat, which perhaps I ought to send to you. It
looked horrid—but somehow I can't feel much interest
in it, or that these curry-combings matter much. So
much more worthwhile, and *far* more humbling, but to
keep on trying to look at Christ. I know instantly by that,
when I do anything odious. Even before Holy
Communion, I don't do much else, but, as it were, let
that love flow over and obliterate everything. There is so
little difference between one's *best* and *worst.*

Probably I ought to tell you this. Last October, one day
when I was praying, quite suddenly a voice seemed to
speak to me—with tremendous staccato sharpness and
clearness. It only said one short thing—first in Latin and
then in English! *Please* don't think I am going in for
psychic automatisms or horrors of that sort. It has never
happened again and I don't want it to. Of course I know
all about the psychological aspect and am not
*hallucinated.* All the same, I simply cannot believe that
there was not something deeper, more real, not me at
all, behind. The effect was terrific. Sort of nailed me to
the floor for half-an-hour, which went in a flash. I felt
definitely called-out and settled, once for all—that any
falling-back or leaving-off after that will be an unpardon-
able treason. This sense has persisted—it marked a sort

of turning-point and the end of all the remorse and worry and feverish banging about. I feel now, if all consolations went, it ought not to matter very much: though as a matter of fact, derelictions are more painful and trying than they used to be, but have their purifying side. I feel a total, unconditioned dedication is what is asked and it is *so* difficult. I shall never do it—one fails at every corner.

There have been other things since, from time to time, but quite formless and unspeakably sacred, penetrating, intimate, abasing. Now and then new lights too, sort of intellectual intuitions and quite clear of "sensible devotion"; but they are so quick and vast one can only retain about half. I would like, in a way, to get away from the more vividly emotional feelings: I don't altogether trust them—but how *can* one help feeling pretty intensely? One has only one soul and body to do one's feeling with after all!

3. Prayer at good times, though still mixed, is more passive; a sort of inarticulate communion, or aspirations, often merely one word, over and over. Sometimes I wonder whether this is not too much taking the line of least resistance; but it is so wonderful, sweeps one along into a kind of warm, inhabited darkness and blind joy—but one lives in eternity in that—can't keep at this pitch long, twenty minutes or so.

I do try to say a few psalms each day and do inter-cessions, but one forgets everything then. Of course it is not always like this, often all distraction and difficulty. As to Intercessions, if I asked myself whether I would face *complete* spiritual deprivation for the good of another— e.g., to effect a conversion—I can't do that yet. So I have not got real Christian love: and the question is, *can* one intercede genuinely for anyone, unless ready to pay, if necessary, this price?

4. *Special Points*

(a) A terrible, overwhelming suspicion that after all

my whole "invisible experience" may only be
subjective. There are times (of course when one
has got it) when it seems incredible these things
*could* happen to me, considering what I have
been. All the books say in unmortified beginners
they are *very suspicious*—so what is one to think?
And further, there is the obvious fact that
consolation and deprivation *are* somehow indeed
closely connected with the ups and downs of
one's nervous and even bodily life. There is no
real test: I may have deceived myself right
through, and, always studying these things, self-
suggestion would be horribly easy. These doubts
are absolute torture, after what has happened.
They paralyse one's life at the roots, once they
lodge in the mind. I do not want to shirk *any* pain
but this does not seem a purifying kind. I have
read over and over all you say in the *Mystical
Element*—one must have suffering and in a way I
wish for it. You state the whole problem there,
but I don't get any certitude for myself. The one
hopeful side is, what happens, though recog-
nizable, does not really match the books; it does
seem my own, yet *infinitely* transcending
anything I could have imagined for myself—and
grows in depth, mystery and sweetness.

You said the first time of all, it *was* all right, I need
have no doubts. You know me better now—if you
could and would say you *still* feel absolutely sure,
I think I could accept that once for all and turn
my back on these horrors whenever they come.
So far, I have struggled through all right, generally
by deliberate, forced prayer—but this only shelves
the problem, doesn't solve it—and all makes one
feel horribly unsafe. The return to peace and
certitude is wonderful: but *how* am I to know for
certain this is not just some psychic mechanism?
There are times when I wish I had never heard of
psychology.

(b) Sometimes an even more terrifying visitation,
when not *only* my own inner experience, but the
whole spiritual scheme seems in question. The
universe seems cast iron and the deterministic

view the obvious one. All the old difficulties come
back; and especially that chasm between the
universal and the historic experience of Christ. I
see that for me, religious realism is the *only* thing
that is any use. Generally I seem to have it with an
increasingly vivid sense of real approach to or
communion with God and Christ as objective
facts, completely other than myself. I can't love on
any other basis than this: even human love can't
be spun from one's dreams, and this is far, far
beyond that. But in these black times of doubt, it
seems possible that one's hours of prayer and
adoration simply react on oneself and produce the
accompanying experiences. I have no guarantee
of genuineness. It is not the awful moral struggle I
knew I should have once I gave in; but that has a
sort of joy in it—these mental conflicts are just
pure horror.

5. *Mortification*. I still feel I ought to do something
about this, partly for love, partly as a training for
suffering: *years* of softness to make up for. But I don't
know the right principle: the books seem to conflict.
Father Doyle's *agere contra* in everything, even
trifles, seems fussy and self-occupied, e.g., always
looking out for an opportunity of doing or even eating
something you don't like! I simply couldn't be
bothered! The other idea, doing and accepting what
comes and never deflecting for one's own likes and
dislikes, seems better and far from easy, but perhaps
not quite *enough*. But so far, you have almost
encouraged me to do things I liked?—"non-religious
interests," etc. Like the comfortable camel in
Ferishtah-bit of chervil and all—but I have a sneaking
sympathy for the other camel! Please would you give
me some direction about all this?

6. *Psycho-Psychic tangles*. The parallels between
nervous states and spiritual sensitiveness worry me
so: nerves and soul seem hopelessly mixed up; one
thinks one is out of grace and finds it was only mental
fatigue and impotence. Don't know how best to run
(my) devotional life in nervous exhaustion. Often too

stupefied to think, will, or love at all. I *do* keep my
whole rule somehow—merely kneeling on a hard
floor the proper time seems better than nothing—but
the struggle to pray is fruitless then.

7. The *Rule-keeping* tends to a sort of rigidity. I am
restless and starved when my particular routine is
upset. And, during holidays, or when travelling,
lecturing, etc.—approximately a quarter of the year—
I can't rely on keeping it. Often no privacy, no certain
free time safe from interruption: and the desperate
struggle to get it at all costs induces a strain which is
hostile to prayer. Lately in fact, "holidays" have been
particular periods of misery on this account. Of
course I *never* sacrifice Communions unless they are
quite impossible—and even these I cannot be sure of
when we are yachting . . . What I want here is
permission to be more flexible about the eternal rule
and make up by taking every opportunity of quietude
or of short aspirations for any irregularity in long
recollections. I believe I should do better like this and
am sure it would not mean slackness. And there must
be some way of supernaturalizing one's active life
when one *can't* have one's usual solitude and fixed
adoration. After all, it is not my choice that I have to
be at other people's disposal the whole time. Could
one not turn these conditions into something worth
offering?

8. *Retreat.* May I go to two three-day retreats in the year
instead of the one whole week retreat, which you
allowed but which is difficult to manage? *Please* say
yes to this! It is such a help and refreshment, in one's
driving, incessantly active life! I come back completely
renovated. But a year between is a very long time to
wait.

9. *Vocation.* I feel a great uncertainty as to what God
chiefly wants of me as to vocation. Selection has
become inevitable. I can't meet more than half the
demands made. I asked for more opportunity of
personal service and have thoroughly been taken at

my word! But there is almost no time or strength now for study for its own sake—always giving or preparing addresses, advice, writing articles, trying to keep pace with work, going on committees and conferences—and with so little mental food—I risk turning into a sort of fluid clergyman! More serious, the conflict between family claims and perhaps duties and work is getting acute. My parents are getting old: they don't understand and are a bit jealous of the claims on my life, especially as it's all unpaid work! I feel perhaps I ought to have more leisure for them, though I do see them nearly every day. But this could only be done by reducing what seems direction work for God, or my poor people or something. I confess the work and poor people are congenial, and idling about chatting and being amiable, when there is so much to be done, a most difficult discipline—so I cannot judge the situation fairly. It is not a case of being needed in any practical sense; but of one's presence being liked and one's other duties slightly resented!

10. *Disobedience.* When I have been alone and had the opportunity, I have sometimes gone to Holy Communion oftener than you said. Otherwise believe I have kept on my collar and chain.

11. *Guilds of Prayer.* Constantly being urged to join Guilds of Prayer, Intercession, etc., and reproached for refusal. Ought I to? I do want so to keep free and hidden in prayer: feel very reluctant to take on these extra rules—but don't wish to be unsocial!

# NOTES

## INTRODUCTION

1. T. S. Eliot, MS A. ff. 90, 91. Cited in H. Garnder, *The Composition of Four Quartets* (London: Faber and Faber, 1978), 69–70.

2. "E. Stuart Moore—Obituary," *The Times* (London), 19 June 1941, p. 7, col. 4.

3. John Macquarrie, *Twentieth Century Religious Thought* (London: SCM, 1981), 408-09.

4. Michael Ramsey, Foreword, in C. Armstrong, *Evelyn Underhill* (Grand Rapids, MI: Eerdmans, 1975), x.

5. M. Cropper, *Evelyn Underhill* (London: Longmans, Green, and Co., 1958), 6.

6. Ibid., 5.

7. Ibid., 13.

8. Lucy Menzies, Biography of Evelyn Underhill, unfinished typescript, St. Andrews University Archives, St. Andrews, Scotland, II, 11.

9. Evelyn Underhill, "A Defence of Magic," *Fortnightly Review* 88 (November 1907): 763–64.

10. Evelyn Underhill, *Mysticism: A Study in the Nature and Development of Man's Spiritual Consciousness* (London: Methuen, 1911), 97.

11. Evelyn Underhill "To F. H.," 20 March 1933, in *The Letters of Evelyn Underhill*, ed., C. Williams (London: Longmans, Green, and Co., 1943), 210.

12. Evelyn Underhill, *The Spiritual Life* (Harrisburg, PA: Morehouse Publishing, 1984), 32.

13. Evelyn Underhill, *School of Charity: Meditations on the Christian Creed* (Harrisburg, PA: Morehouse Publishing, 1990), 14.

14. Evelyn Underhill, *Concerning the Inner Life*, (1926; Minneapolis: Seabury Press, 1984), l05.

15. Ibid., 150–51.

16. Underhill, *The Spiritual Life*, 80–81.

17. Evelyn Underhill, "To Maisie Spens," All Saints 1940, Letters, 296–97.

18. Evelyn Underhill, "To E. I. Watkin," 27 April 1941, Letters, 305.

### INTRODUCTION TO THE GREEN NOTEBOOK, 1923–24

1. Friedrich von Hügel to Mrs. Stuart Moore, 26 June 1916, Evelyn Underhill Collection (EUC), Archives, King's College, London, folder 46.

2. The typescripts of these letters are in the Von Hügel-Underhill Collection, St. Andrews University Archives, St. Andrews, Scotland.

3. Lucy Menzies, Biography of Evelyn Underhill, ix, 22.

4. Evelyn Underhill, "Baron von Hügel as a Spiritual Teacher," in *Mixed Pasture*, (London: Methuen, 1933), 230.

5. "To Dom Chapman," 9 June 1931, in *Letters*, 196.

6. Von Hügel to Underhill, late 1921, Von Hügel-Underhill Collection.

7. Gwendolyn Greene, Introduction, in *Letters from Baron Friedrich von Hügel to a Niece* (London: J. M. Dent, 1928), xii.

8. C. Williams, Introduction, in *Letters*, 26.

9. Von Hügel to Underhill, 12 July 1923, von Hügel-Underhill Collection.

10. Underhill to von Hügel, midsummer 1922, von Hügel-Underhill Collection.

11. Von Hügel to Underhill, end of 1921, von Hügel-Underhill Collection.

12. Ibid.

13. "To F. H.," 11 May 1933, *Letters*, 211.

14. "To F. H.," 2O Mar. 1933, *Letters*, 211.

15. Evelyn Underhill, "The Authority of Personal Religious Experience," *Theology* 10, no. 55 (January 1925): 13.

## THE GREEN NOTEBOOK, 1923–24

1. This 1924 retreat and those for 1925, 1927, and 1928 have been published as *The Ways of the Spirit,* edited and with an introduction by Grace Adolphsen Brame (New York: Crossroad, 1990). See also F. Campbell, "Evelyn Underhill: Conversion at Pleshey," *The Living Church,* 1 March 1987, 11–13.
2. Evelyn Underhill, "Worship," in *Collected Papers* (London: Longmans, Green and Co., 1946), 92. Emphasis added.
3. Arthur Underhill, *Change and Decay: The Recollections and Reflections of an Octogenarian Bencher* (London: Butterworth and Co., 1938), 211.
4. Underhill to von Hügel, 21 Dec. 1921, von Hügel-Underhill Collection.
5. Von Hügel, *Letters from Baron Friedrich von Hügel to a Niece.*
6. "To Lucy Menzies," 2 Aug. 1924, *Letters,* 323.

## INTRODUCTION TO THE GREEN AND FLOWERED NOTEBOOKS, 1926–37

1. The brief extant correspondence between them is contained in *The Spiritual Letters of Dom John Chapman* (London: Sheed and Ward, 1935), 107.
2. Lucy Menzies to Gillian (Wilkinson), 17 Jan. ( no year), EUC, Archives, King's College, London, folder 37.
3. Ibid.
4. R.S.Ward, *A Guide for Spiritual Directors* (London: Mowbray, 1957).
5. "To L. M.," July 1929, *Letters,* 335.
6. "To L. M.," June 1932, *Letters,* 204.
7. Evelyn Underhill, *The Mount of Purification* (New York: David McKay Co., 1960), 16.
8. Ibid., 10.
9. Ibid., 64.
10. Ibid.
11. Evelyn Underhill, *The Golden Sequence: A Four-fold Study of the Spiritual Life* (London; Methuen, 1932), 114.
12. "To G. F.," Sept. 1937, *Letters,* 260.
13. "To L. M.," Eve of Annunciation 1938, *Letters,* 339.
14. "To L. M.," Trinity VI 1938, *Letters,* 340.
15. Sister Mary of St. John to Evelyn Underhill, 23 Feb. 1939, EUC, folder 45.

5819